Thinking Through
Script Analysis

Thinking Through
Script Analysis

Suzanne Burgoyne, Ph.D.
University of Missouri

Patricia Downey
University of South Dakota

Thinking Through Script Analysis

Focus Publishing/R. Pullins Company
PO Box 369
Newburyport, MA 01950
www.focusbookstore.com

Illustration/Photo/Text Credits:

Cover photo	©University of Missouri
p. 8	©Kathy Konkle/iStock Photo
p. 43, 94	Illustrations by Caroline J. Potter
p. 56	©2011 Estate of Pablo Picasso/Artists Rights Society (ARS) New York; Photo credit: Reunion des Musées Nationaux/Art Resource NY
pp. 38–42	Excerpt from *Sophocles' King Oidipous* translated by Ruby Blondell. ©2002, Focus Publishing/ R. Pullins Co., Inc. Used by permission.
p. 84–85, 141–143	Excerpts from Moliere's *Tartuffe*, translated by Morris Bishop, ed. by Kenneth J. Rivers. Used by permission.
p. 125	©Eiji Ueda/iStock Photo
p. 152, 153	Costume drawings by James M. Miller, Professor of Theatre, University of Missouri
p. 154, 155	Photos ©University of Missouri

ISBN 13: 978-1-58510-361-4

11 10 9 8 7 6 5 4 3 2

Last updated December 2011

Table of Contents

How do I decide if it's the major crisis or the major climax?
  Exercise 3:4 Paradigm shift
  Example 3:1 Thinking through key structural elements of *Avatar*
What are the criteria for structural analysis?
Capstone Assignment: Structural Analysis

What is a Root Action Statement (RAS)?
How is an RAS structured?
  Exercise 4:1 Creating a story-level RAS
What is 'Abstraction'?
  Exercise 4:2 Abstracting in daily life
How do you apply abstraction to script analysis?
  Example 4:1 Abstracting up from story-level
How do you write an RAS?
  Example 4:2 Refining the description of the protagonist
  Exercise 4:3 Describing yourself as protagonist
How do I unify an RAS?
  Example 4:3 Analyzing an RAS for unity
How does the RAS relate to the script's meaning?
  Exercise 4:4 Thinking about themes
  Example 4:4 Working on an RAS for *Avatar*
  Exercise 4:5 Comparing the RAS to your interpretation of the
      meaning of the script?
What are the criteria for writing an effective RAS?
  Exercise 4:6 Using the criteria to evaluate and revise your sample RAS
Capstone Assignment: RAS and Structural Analysis

What kinds of thinking do actors use to create characters?
What are character spines?
What is the format for a spine?
Why verbs?
Which kinds of verbs are weak?
What kinds of verbs are actable?
  Exercise 5:1 Strengthening your verb choices
  Exercise 5:2 Theory into Practice: playing your verb choices.
How does an actor create character spines?
  Exercise 5:3 Using the RAS as a jumping off point for developing
      character spines.
How do I harvest clues from the script?

The main action
Patterns in the script
Title of Script
Philosophical statements by characters in the script
Contradictions and Structural Oddities
Historical Context of *Tartuffe*
What are the criteria for effective thematic statements?
Capstone Assignment: Thematic Statements

What is a Central Production Metaphor?
How does a metaphor work?
Why use a central production metaphor?
Who creates the central production metaphor?
How do I find a central production metaphor?
What are the criteria for a central production metaphor?
Capstone Assignment: Central Production Metaphor

What will I find in the Appendix?
Chapter 3: Action and Structure
Exercises using Kinesthetic (Body) Thinking
Chapter 4: Root Action Statements

List of Illustrations

Foreword
Playing With Plays, Critically

Craig E. Nelson

This book is a delight. It is quite interesting to read — and to think about. It shows students how to think critically while helping them understand the core processes involved in turning a written play (a "script") into performances. And it shows faculty how to translate most of the key ideas about critical thinking into a set of explicit learning tasks and teaching moves. It should be quite useful to faculty in a broad range of disciplines, as it was to me. Indeed, the Preface is titled: "Thinking across the curriculum."

This book is also an excellent model of what course design ought to be, but often is not. Burgoyne and Downey have undertaken two core tasks. They have designed the entire book to teach the disciplinary "content" of script analysis, " how to understand a script in the ways theatre artists analyze it in order to bring the script to life on the stage." But they also have designed the entire book to simultaneously and explicitly use that content to foster higher-level critical thinking skills. This "dual-function" of content both as content and as a vehicle for learning critical thinking challenges students to learn in new ways and challenges faculty to think deeply about the goals they want to achieve with each class-period, assignment and course.

Most importantly, the approach to critical thinking in this book is both innovative and sure to be very effective. Undergraduates typically have two core ways of thinking about content. In a very interesting move, the authors ask the students to see both as misconceptions:

Misconception: There's only one "right meaning," which is what the author "really meant," and it's the teacher's job to tell me what that meaning is.

Misconception: If there is no one "right meaning," then any interpretation must be valid.

Other studies have shown that these two assumptions about knowing predominate among undergraduates, even among seniors. In asking students to see the two as misconceptions, the authors can more easily challenge them explicitly and effectively. As a strong challenge to the first misconception they note: "There is not universal agreement within the discipline" even on terms and definitions. Equally strong challenges are offered for the second: "Not all interpretations are equally valid." And, crucially: "Different artists find different meanings in the same script, so interpretations vary, making space for creativity." The authors also ask the students to watch for these and other misconceptions as they monitor their own and other students' comments on scripts. Treating these ways of thinking as misconceptions also implicitly asks faculty to remember that these ideas are going to be resistant to change and are likely to require the students to engage in several rounds of active reconsideration. Simply telling a student what is wrong with a misconception is rarely adequate to transform it into a more useful view.

The overall approach is focused on moving students from these two misconceptions into a third core way of thinking, one that empowers them to compare alternative interpretations and decide which is preferable on a number of criteria. This third way can best be learned first within a single discipline. Here: "We want to help you discover how to understand a script in the ways theatre artists analyze it in order to bring the script to life on the stage." And, again, any interpretation must be grounded first of all in what is actually in the text: "A valid interpretation requires skill in both analytical and critical thinking. You also need to support your ideas with evidence from the script." The text provides great mnemonics to help students avoid some common interpretive problems (including "textual narcissism," "Freudian snooping" and "grabbing a tree and forgetting the forest"). The development of such mnemonics is a technique that should be widely emulated by other faculty.

The analytical framework the authors have formulated explicitly applies to scripts that have a traditional, linear, cause/effect structure. Other frameworks, such as feminism, are set aside as best addressed in subsequent courses. The choice to set more complex approaches temporarily aside is an exceptionally good one. It is very hard for students to learn to use multiple frameworks accurately before they have a deep mastery of at least one specific framework. Further, a script with a linear cause/effect structure can be analyzed largely on its own terms. Frameworks such as feminism are more complicated as they require a mastery of complex ideas that are much more external to the script. Typically they also elicit or require a deep rethinking of the student's own values. These are tasks best left to the next stage of critical thinking, one that depends on first having a solid mastery of at least one and, ideally, two or more analytical frameworks.

It is not easy for students to move from the two common core misconceptions about how to think to a new way of thinking, one that is focused on thinking with and in an analytical framework. One key problem is that it takes a lot more effort to understand things in this new way of thinking. Hence, the authors challenge another key "misconception" (number one in their list). This misconception is the idea, common among students, that plays can be understood by skimming rather than by close reading. Instead, you must actually read the text and think about it in ways that allow you to "examine its structure and unpack its deeper meanings." Most importantly, you must figure out what the characters are thinking as the script typically doesn't make this explicit. Worse, from the students' perspective, "prying into characters' minds requires multiple readings of the script."

Just as the students need to work harder to master the new ways of thinking, faculty have to work differently to support the students' progress and to make fostering critical thinking central to learning. A lot of support is required if students are to meet this challenge. The authors call one major set of supports "scaffolding." Their efforts here include:

- Modeling how an experienced script analyst thinks with a focus on two example scripts,
- Asking students to apply skills to examples from everyday life with a focus on the individual student's interests,
- Asking students to master and apply new skills sequentially before asking them to use the new skills in combination in the capstone assignments for each chapter,
- Providing resources and encouragement for students to work

together at key points in their learning (faculty who adopt this approach would be well advised to require such group work),

- Asking students to adopt a "mental management" approach (structured, intentional metacognition) both generally and as they learn to do analytical and creative thinking.

To help students (and faculty) integrate and apply this dual function approach, Burgoyne and Downey ask students to differentiate among four developmentally different approaches to "critical thinking," approaches based ultimately on Perry's analyses. For these developmental differences they have invented labels that will resonate well with the students' backgrounds.

- Colonel Quaritch (a character from *Avatar*): Only one "right meaning" (the first core misconception).
- "Whatever!": "Any interpretation must be valid" in the face of uncertainty (the second core misconception).
- Basketball vs Quidditch: This is the central content/thinking approach of the book ("to understand a script in the ways theatre artists analyze it ") generalized to asking within any specific context "On what grounds, or according to what *criteria*, does one evaluate the various alternatives?" "*It is in this stage that a student actually begins to engage in critical thinking.*" This is the approach needed for analysis of the scripts treated in this book (again, those that have a traditional, linear, cause/effect structure.)
- Choosing your own golden snitch: Here one chooses how to think and act using the critical thinking developed in the preceding approach in combination with one's own values and with a comparison among contexts. This approach would be needed later for some of the kinds of scripts set aside here as best addressed in advanced courses.

In summary, this book illustrates an important approach to helping students more deeply master some key goals of undergraduate education: close reading, critical thinking, effective writing, productive group work and "mental management." Readers will find it interesting to see how these themes and tools are applied throughout the book. Enjoy.

Craig E Nelson is an Emeritus Professor of Biology at Indiana. He was named *The Outstanding Research and Doctoral Universities Professor of the Year 2000* by the Carnegie Foundation for the Advancement of Teaching & Council for the Advancement and Support of Education. He was founding president of the International Society for the Scholarship of Teaching and Learning. His teaching papers address critical thinking, mature valuing, diversity, active learning, teaching evolution and the Scholarship of Teaching and Learning. His biological research was on evolution and ecology.

Acknowledgements

Having taught and practiced script analysis — as an actor and director — for over thirty years, I need to point out that many sources have contributed to my understanding of this demanding art. Some sources are credited in the text. Others include colleagues, as passionate as I about the intricacies of analysis, who gifted me with their ideas. During the past twenty years, I have benefited from the invaluable contributions of generations of graduate student teaching assistants, who asked thought-provoking questions and uncomplainingly helped grade reams of papers. And then there are the hundreds of undergraduate students whose struggles provoked me to wrestle with my own thinking processes so I could make those processes transparent — and whose triumphant "aha!" moments filled me with delight. You all know who you are, and I thank you all. Finally, a bow of thanks to the student who asked, "Couldn't you take a well-known film and walk us through the process of analyzing it?" To you I owe the pleasure of my close encounter with *Avatar*. Thanks to Ron Pullins, who made me think again about some of my choices and whose willingness to support a somewhat "out of the box" book renews my faith in publishers. Most of all, I thank Patricia Downey, my co-author. Patricia's insights and insistence that every point we make be crystal clear forced me to probe more deeply into my own thought processes and discover why I was doing things I didn't realize I was doing. Patricia's abilities complement mine so beautifully, making our work on the book a true collaboration. Her integrity and honesty, as well as her support and enthusiasm, gave me joy.

S.B.

My contribution to this text would not have been possible without the mentoring, scholarship, and inspiration provided by many, many others. First, I want to thank my mentors at the University of Missouri-Columbia (MU): Dr. Cheryl Black, Dr. Suzanne Burgoyne, Dr. Mary Heather Carver, Dr. David Crespy, Dr. Weldon Durham in the Department of Theatre, Dr. Jeni Hart, in the Department of Educational Leadership and Policy Analysis and Dr. Marilyn Miller, former Director of the Program for Excellence in Teaching. Each of these educators generously supported, encouraged, and guided my work as a scholar/artist at MU. Second, I want to acknowledge my indebtedness to all those scholar/teachers who share their work through the Scholarship of Teaching and Learning. Dr. Ernest Boyer, Dr. Arthur Costa, Dr. Bena Kallick, Dr. Arthur Levine, Dr. Ron Ritchhart, and Dr. Maryellen Weimer are just a few of the many scholars whose ideas awakened my curiosity and spoke to my heart about student-centered teaching. Third, a big thank you goes out to my current and past students who challenge(d) me daily to be a co-learner in the classroom with them and taught me so much. I am also grateful for the many times students and faculty colleagues at the University of South Dakota have stopped by my office to inquire, "How is the book coming along?" and "What is it about?" Each query has engaged me anew in the work and helped me clarify my thinking. Finally, I want to thank Dr. Suzanne Burgoyne for inviting me to share in the gloriously creative experience of writing this book. She is my friend, my mentor, and my inspiration. Suzanne is the artist/scholar/teacher I aspire to become. Thank you, Suzanne, for the opportunity and the challenge this process brought into my life. I am blessed by your guidance and friendship

P.D.

Preface
Thinking Across the Curriculum

In a new play, "Holding Up the Sky," storyteller Milbre Burch refers to a folk tale in which an elephant comes across a tiny hummingbird lying on its back with its legs sticking up in the air. The elephant asks the hummingbird what it's doing, and the bird replies that the sky is falling. "And you think your little feet can hold up the sky?" the elephant laughs. "No," the hummingbird says stoutly, "but I'm doing what I can."

The world is changing so dizzyingly fast it's hard to keep up. Much subject matter information goes out of date before a student can even take the exam. Numerous visionaries call for higher education to prepare our students not only to survive but to flourish in a complex, ever-changing environment. As Norman Jackson points out in "Imagining a Different World," employers expect graduates to emerge from the university with high-level thinking skills in various areas. Scholars such as Jackson and Joanne Kurfiss, in her book *Critical Thinking*, call for schools to develop programs to teach thinking skills across the curriculum.

Intention

How many things do you know that are "just one thing"? Almost everything in our lives serves more than one purpose, often simultaneously. A car can simultaneously be a means of transportation and an object of aesthetic pleasure. A book can both explore great ideas and entertain us. Can a course teach disciplinary content and higher-level thinking skills at the same time? We've designed this book according to our belief that it can.

Maryellen Weimer, in *Learner-Centered Teaching,* calls this model of course design the "Dual-Function of Content." Such courses strive to bring the learner to a level of disciplinary expertise while at the same time intentionally and transparently developing higher-level thinking skills. The disciplinary content serves as material upon which the learner can practice particular thinking skills. Weimer notes that combining content with the intentionality of teaching thinking complicates learning in a good way. It creates a synergy that causes each to be more effective than either would be alone.

The Dual-Function of Content model of course design puts visibility of thinking front and center. We have intentionally designed exercises, examples, models, and assignments that will challenge student and teacher to think about their thinking. In this text we focus on developing analytical, creative, and critical thinking through the process of script analysis. All three are essential thinking skills for theatre artists, skills which transfer to other problem-solving endeavors. The text thus serves as a practical guide for undergraduate and graduate students who hope for a career in theatre but also for readers from other disciplines seeking to sharpen their thinking.

In order to embed in our text activities that stimulate high-level thinking, we needed to know what kinds of attitudes, behaviors, and skills make such thinking visible. The work of Arthur Costa and Bena Kallick proved essential to our understanding of sixteen intellectual habits they identify as "Habits of Mind (HOM)." Costa defines an HOM as a disposition or attitude signaling intelligent behavior when a person is confronted with a problem to which he does not have a ready answer, problems like paradoxes, dilemmas, enigmas and uncertainties. A person who has developed these dispositions recognizes that knowledge, once acquired, must be tested, reflected upon, adapted, and developed in order to seed the creation of something new. HOM transfer across disciplinary boundaries and are the intellectual characteristics of people who are successful in both their personal and professional lives.

Costa and Kallick remind us that HOM do not function in isolation from one another. There is a subtle interplay among them in the process of successful problem-solving. HOM work in clusters and adapt to various contexts. For a more extensive discussion of habits of mind please refer to the Habits of Mind website address in our bibliography.

Underpinnings: hopes and concerns emerging from neuroscience

Neuroscience and MRI scanning are adding to our knowledge of how the brain works. A new interdisciplinary field is emerging to bring together education, brain science, and other subject areas to explore how new discoveries can improve teaching and learning for everyone. Ideas from this emerging field provide a foundation for our approach — including the belief that people actually can improve their thinking skills, as well as a concern that deep understanding may disappear from the repertoire of human abilities if we humans don't practice high-level thinking skills.

Brain science is still in relatively early stages but so far there seems to be good news and bad news. The good news is that the brain can change, creating new networks and learning new skills. According to neuroscientists Mary Helen Immordino-Yang and Kurt Fischer, brain research demonstrates that biology is not destiny when it comes to the ability of a child to learn, that biology, culture, and experience interact to shape an individual. The bad news? Brain science warns that if we don't continually challenge our "brain muscles" by learning new and difficult skills that require hard work, those new cells just die.

Judith Horstman, in *The Scientific American Brave New Brain,* also raises the question whether our ever-expanding immersion in digital technology is good or bad for our brains. Some positive indications include the growth of interactive learning, enhanced visual senses, and greater speed in shifting attention. The concerns have to do with loss of ability to concentrate and weaker skills at social interaction such as loss of ability to read non-verbal signals. Plus some studies suggest that the fast neural shifting correlates with a rise in ADHD. Nicholas Carr, author of *The Shallows,* worries not only about how addictive web activities are but that the changes in our brains may lead to an evolutionary transformation such that the human race will no longer be capable of deep and sustained thinking.

Scope of the text

The approach to script analysis we present in this book works for scripts with traditional, linear cause/effect structure. This type of dramatic structure still predominates in Western culture in spite of avant-garde experimentation. We confine our scope not only because the majority of scripts fit the linear pattern but because we believe one needs to grasp traditional structure before grappling with non-traditional scripts. It's easier to figure out how and why a script deviates from traditional structure if one knows what traditional structure is. Similarly, our analytic approach grows out of realistic, Stanislavski-based acting — and for the same reasons. We suggest that important topics such as non-realistic style and structure, including feminist script writing, would best be addressed in an advanced script analysis course for students who have mastered the skills in this book.

Methods of instruction

Since part of our goal is to make thinking visible, we want to make visible the patterns of instruction we have used to organize this text. Pattern recognition itself is an essential intellectual behavior that we will explore when we search for patterns in a script.

We believe the text will be more useful if we make the overall organization transparent.

Scaffolding

One teaching/learning method we use extensively is called **scaffolding.** Scaffolding is based on the constructivist theory of knowledge: students build on what they already know to develop new concepts and skills. Thus scaffolding involves a number of activities that help students construct a mental bridge from what they already know to what they want to learn. While the idea of "scaffolding" has many implications, we feature several elements prominently:

1. According to developmental psychologist Lev Vygotsky, people learn best when engaging in social interaction. The student serves as an apprentice to someone more experienced in the field, who guides, models, demonstrates, creates learning activities and evaluation rubrics, and gives feedback. In this book, we've included guidance, activities, examples, standards, rubrics, and modeling of how an experienced script analyst thinks. The scripts for *Oedipus Rex* by Sophocles, *Tartuffe* by Molière, *Arms and the Man* by George Bernard Shaw, and the film *Avatar* by James Cameron are analyzed by our experienced script analyst and shared throughout the text. Students who see the film and read the scripts multiple times will benefit most from the course.

2. Since scaffolding helps students build on what they already know, we provide exercises in which students are asked to apply particular skills to things from everyday life before tackling a script.

3. Scaffolding also helps motivate students by showing how the course material relates to the student's life. We make connections between students' interests and the skills we encourage. Students only learn deeply when they really want to.

4. Scaffolding allows students to learn in digestible bites by offering activities in which they practice skills one by one. Each chapter contains a capstone assignment and accompanying criteria designed to allow students to integrate the bites. Additionally, the information the student creates in a capstone provides the scaffolding for the next chapter.

5. Because of the social learning emphasis, scaffolding often involves students in group learning activities, such as peer review and group projects. Most of the exercises we propose can be done alone, but we encourage group work. Students will find in Appendix B a "Peer Review Checklist" to accompany the capstone assignment. We encourage students to empower themselves by seeking targeted feedback from one another.

The underlying metaphor of educational scaffolding is, of course, the scaffolding that surrounds a building while it's being constructed. After each part is finished, the scaffolding is taken down. Similarly, educational scaffolding supports the student while she's just a beginner then is removed to allow the student to stand on her own two feet, capable of directing her ongoing learning.

Organization of the Text

Course instructors know the needs of their students better than anyone else. We've embedded in the text an array of scaffolding exercises and examples. The choice of *which* exercises to use or *whether* to use them at all is up to the instructor and the individual student. Some instructors may have their own library of preferred exercises and assignments. Likewise, instructors may choose to skip entire chapters. We have formatted the book so that exercises may be easily identified by the reader and utilized or discarded at the discretion of the instructor and student.

Terminology

Like other subject fields, theatre employs specialized terms. There is not universal agreement within the discipline, however, on all terms and definitions. What one actor may call a "spine," another may call a "superobjective." What one director might refer to as a "beat," another might term a "unit." The glossary to this book defines each term as used in this text. As each new term appears for the first time it will be shown in **bold type**, alerting the student that it is in the glossary. When communicating with theatre artists outside of this class, we suggest. minimizing confusion by making sure everyone understands the terms being used.

Content Organized Around Questions

We have framed the content of each chapter with basic questions such as What, When, Who, Where, Why, and How. This framing device gives the reader a specific purpose on which to focus within each section of a chapter, consequently increasing comprehension. Section questions highlight the major points to be covered in a chapter and help the student differentiate between the thesis of a section and the explanatory details.

A final thought

Stories and theatre performances may not save the world overnight, but they certainly can stimulate thinking. The better theatre artists understand the scripts they're staging, the more the performances can touch the hearts and minds of audiences. We're not trying to hold up the sky with this book, but like the hummingbird, we're doing the best we can.

Chapter 1
Getting Started: Thinking About Thinking

So how do we start?

A good place to start any learning process is to identify goals. Our first goal is to help you discover how to understand a **script** in the ways theatre artists analyze it in order to bring the script to life on the stage. A related goal is to give you practice in thinking strategies needed to unearth and embody the soul of the story. Thus our goals are practical and artistic. The thinking skills involved are also valuable for such everyday purposes as living, learning, and earning. Let's get started by doing a brief exercise in thinking.

Lift the hand that's not holding the book and look at it. Really look at it. Isn't the human hand an amazing thing? It allows us to touch and experience textures from sharp thorns to silky fur. It's a tool that enables us to accomplish a huge range of tasks. It's a means of connecting with another human being. Furthermore, we can teach our hands to acquire new skills, if we take the time to learn and practice. How often do we think about how our hands work? Do we take them for granted? Likewise, how often do we think about how our thinking works? Do we take our thinking for granted?

EXERCISE 1:1
Stop and think

STOP! What thought just went through your mind in response to the sentence before "stop!" Write that thought down. We'll be coming back to it after you've read the chapter.

1

In this chapter, we'll introduce you to some thinking tools you'll need in order to get the most out of this textbook. Let's get started by looking at another activity we sometimes take for granted: reading.

How do you read a script?

Is reading a script different from reading a novel? A news story? A letter from a loved one? In what ways?

A script is a special kind of writing. It's written to be read by a team of **artistic collaborators** who will transform it into a living, breathing, three-dimensional entity: a **play**. In this book, we distinguish between the written and the performed text by using the term "script" for the first and "play" for the second. Like the DNA contained in a seed, a script contains information essential to its flowering into performance. The script's DNA is coded in patterns of words and silences, action, metaphors, visual images, themes, internal structure, and overall form. Theatre artists decode the DNA by recognizing these patterns. In this book, we share with you the decoding tools artists use to analyze a script. The decoded information allows you to cultivate your unique artistic interpretation.

Phenomenologist Bruce Wilshire compares theatre to a scientist's laboratory, a place to explore the question: what does it mean to be human? Playwrights encode various aspects of that question, and sometimes partial answers, in their scripts. What theatre artists mean by "an **interpretation**" is an experience created for audiences. An interpretation communicates an artistic team's vision of what the script shows regarding the meaning of human life. A **"valid" interpretation** is grounded in what's actually in the script. Different artists find different meanings in the same script, so interpretations vary, making space for creativity. **Script analysis** allows artists to decode the script in ways that help them make artistic choices leading to a valid interpretation. But before you can develop an interpretation, you have to learn to read the code.

Because scripts are a special kind of writing, reading them calls for special reading and thinking skills. You may be tempted to say, "I've been reading and thinking most of my life; how different can this script stuff be?" Our preconceptions and reading habits can block us from learning new ways of thinking. Let's take a quick look at some common habits that lead to misconceptions about reading literature (including scripts). If any of these mistaken ideas sound like something you might have believed before taking this class, put a checkmark beside them. If you find similar thoughts popping into your head during the semester, please recognize them as pesky misconceptions and shoo them out of your way, freeing your mind to fly.

Misconception: I'm used to skimming textbooks and web pages for important points, so I can read scripts that way, too.

To understand any work of literature, you have to read closely. When you read something *closely,* you examine its structure and unpack its deeper meanings. Scripts require even more thorough reading than novels because the playwright doesn't tell you what the characters are thinking — you need to "read their actions" to figure out what's going on in their heads. Prying into characters' minds requires multiple readings of the script.

Misconception: I've learned how to multi-task, so I can read a script at the same time I'm doing other things.

Sorry, but recent scientific research shows that "multi-tasking" is a myth. When someone multi-tasks s/he changes focus mentally from one thing to another, destroying concentration and fragmenting the learning experience. Multi-tasking actually makes learning more difficult if not impossible. As we've said above, scripts require close reading, and close reading requires concentration. You can't read the script in bits and pieces; you need time and quiet surroundings to enter imaginatively into the script's world. Even soft music might distract you by evoking a mood different from the ones evoked by the script. Read without interruption to understand the script fully.

Misconception: There's only one "right meaning," which is what the author "really meant," and it's the teacher's job to tell me what that meaning is.

There isn't only one "right meaning." If the teacher just tells you her favorite interpretation, you won't learn how to analyze scripts. You also won't be exercising your thinking skills if you accept at face value someone else's ideas. There is an old saying, "Feed a man a fish and you feed him for a day; teach a man to fish and you feed him for a lifetime." We want to develop "fishers" of ideas rather than consumers of canned tuna.

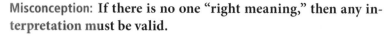

Misconception: If there is no one "right meaning," then any interpretation must be valid.

Not all interpretations are equally valid. A valid interpretation requires skill in both analytical and critical thinking. You also need to support your ideas with evidence from the script. See listed below the thinking habits we advise you to avoid; they can lead toward unsupportable interpretations.

1. **Stating the obvious**. Beware of paraphrasing or re-stating what a character says or does. Such information can be supporting evidence but by itself isn't an interpretation.
2. **Shut-down readings**. Beware of settling for the quick and easy moral lesson or cliché, such as "crime doesn't pay." This type of superficial thinking keeps you from discovering the deeper meanings in the script.
3. **Textual narcissism**. Don't assume all scripts are really about what's going on today in your own culture.
4. **Freudian snooping**. Beware of engaging in unauthorized psychoanalysis of the author or a character with no textual evidence.
5. **Grabbing a tree and forgetting the forest**. Beware of building an interpretation on the basis of one piece of evidence and thereby missing the larger picture.

Misconception: Reading is just for pleasure, and script analysis ruins the experience.

Reading for fun is fine, but if you're part of an artistic team producing a play, you need to understand the script more thoroughly than a casual reader does. You may find that your experience of the script is enhanced by the discoveries you make through analyzing it — and that what you learn about how scripts work will enrich your experience of other scripts on the page or plays on the stage.

The tools presented in this text guide you to read in ways that avoid the pitfalls we have just described. They are designed to enhance the reading experience, to help you uncover the deeper aspects and meanings of a script.

Why do I need to think about thinking?

To succeed in the complex, ever-changing environment of the twenty-first century, today's student must emerge from the university with high-level thinking skills regardless of disciplinary specialty. It's now believed that each individual will change careers (not just jobs) at least five times during her life. The pace of change keeps speeding up: technological change driving social and economic change.

Unfortunately, a recent survey of business leaders (2007-2008) reported that over two-thirds of employers found college graduates lacking in essential intellectual competencies such as analytical, critical, and creative thinking. Fortunately, thinking is a skill. Like other skills, it can be learned.

For years, it was believed that after reaching adulthood, a brain couldn't change. The good news: current neuroscience has revealed that the brain is flexible. It can create new neurons and networks throughout a person's life, allowing changes in behavior, habits, and thinking patterns. You can learn to think in new ways, and to think more effectively in ways you already know.

In *Up and Out: Using Creative and Critical Thinking Skills to Enhance Learning*, Andrew Johnson suggests the best way to teach thinking skills is to practice them while learning a particular subject. We take this approach, giving you exercises in which you apply the high-level thinking skills to script analysis. The thinking skills you strengthen as you learn script analysis can be transferred to other fields. Even if you're not planning a life in theatre, the high-level skills you learn in this course may ultimately help get you a job.

Another means of building thinking skills is for an "expert" in the subject to guide the learner through the thinking process by making her own thinking visible. In the book, we provide demonstrations of an experienced theatre artist thinking through analysis of the film *Avatar* and the scripts *Arms and the Man*, *Oedipus the King*, and *Tartuffe*. Making learning visible is an important method for discovering your own thinking habits. Research shows that students who become aware of their own thinking process and add to their repertoire of thinking strategies are likely to learn better than students who don't. One characteristic of intelligent, successful people is the ability to be mindful of their own thinking habits.

What does it mean to "think about thinking"?

Humans have an amazing ability: we can do something and watch ourselves doing it. We can both think and observe our thinking. Much of our thinking, however, remains invisible to us because we are also creatures of habit. Over time, we become comfortable with our habitual ways of thinking and cease to pay attention to how effective they are. We need to make our thinking visible in order to strengthen what works and discard what doesn't, transfer our thinking skills from one field of study to another, and recognize what we know and don't know.

A scientific term for being mindful of our thinking habits is **metacognition**. "Metacognition" means thinking about how we think, behave, and feel. Tishman, Perkins, and Jay, authors of *The Thinking Classroom*, use the term **mental management**, which implies that we not only *think* about but *guide* our own thinking. We prefer this term also because it captures the essence of the thinking exercises we've embedded in this text. Mental management takes us beyond observation and implies we can act upon our observations to become more effective thinkers.

Thinking Skill #1: Mental Management

There are numerous strategies for managing thinking. You may already have developed your own. Here, we outline a strategy from *The Thinking Classroom* we've adapted to script analysis, but it can also be applied to other tasks. We suggest you try this strategy for the assignments in the book. We include some tools with each assignment to help you think about your thinking.

1. **Prepare your mind to think.** Focus and concentration facilitate effective thinking. Get ready for your task, whether it's reading a script or writing a draft of an analysis, by finding a quiet space free from distractions. Do whatever helps you to attain a state of mind that's relaxed but alert, ready to learn.
2. **Get a plan!** Think ahead about your goals, strategies, and standards so your study time is not wasted. What are you trying to achieve? What strategy works best for your goal? What standards will you use to evaluate whether or not you've achieved your goals?
3. **Monitor your thinking.** Every so often, stop and ask yourself, "How am I doing? Am I making progress towards my goals?

Am I meeting my standards?" If you don't seem to be making good progress, consider what the obstacles are. Are there more effective strategies you could try?

4. **Get a team on your side!** Seek feedback and use the feedback to revise your analysis. Experts in a field often consult with colleagues. There's nothing wrong with asking for responses to your work. With each major assignment we've included a feedback form adapted to that assignment. Your instructor might assign you a peer reviewer, or you might ask a classmate or friend to let you know how you're doing. You could also use the form as a checklist to review your own work. Decide what aspects of the feedback you want to address and make the changes in your next draft.

5. **Reflect on your thinking process!** People who want to excel at any endeavor will take time to reflect on what they've done. We include a "Mental Management" reflection paper with each major assignment and suggest questions to stimulate your thinking.

Mental management is a thinking skill crucial to all higher-order thinking and learning. Remember, you're not only learning about script analysis. You're learning about you and *how* you learn.

Thinking Skill #2: Analytical Thinking

Analysis is a powerful thinking tool. The purpose of **analytical thinking** is to help us understand at a deep level the essential nature of a phenomenon, process, or situation. Analysis allows us to get inside the object of the analysis and see it from many perspectives. When we analyze something we come to know it from the inside out and see how it "works."

The process of analysis has three essential steps: recognition of essential elements, deeper study of each individual element, and development of an understanding of the relationships of the elements to one another and to the whole. By delineating these three steps as essential to the process of analysis we have actually been engaging in the analytical process. We have been analyzing the process of analysis. So how does this process apply to script analysis?

The first step in script analysis is to recognize the kind of information essential to creating an interpretation for the stage. Chapter headings two through seven of this book identify broad categories of information we look for in a script: given circumstances, overall structure of the action, root action of a protagonist, character development, internal structure of scenes, and thematic ideas.

The second step is closer scrutiny of each category. In a sense, we are going to "unpack" each category to get at clues the playwright has packed into the script. When we prepare for a journey we carefully pack suitcases with articles that serve different purposes on our trip. We might pack clothing, toiletries, and devices to entertain us. These articles provide clues to the kind of trip we're taking. In script analysis, authors pack things like images, patterns of actions, and thematic subjects into the script. It is the role and goal of the artistic team to unpack these clues so we can begin to understand the methods this script uses to take us on an emotional and intellectual journey.

The third step, understanding the relationships of the elements to one another and to the whole, requires us to do more than dismantle the script. Discovering the inner relationships of the elements creates a roadmap leading us to our interpretation. In this way we unlock the "magic" of a script in order to create something that exceeds the sum of its parts. Let's try working through the process of analysis with a visual example.

Example 1:1 Unpacking the Process of Analytical Thinking

Figure 1:1
Quilt Block

1. Take a look at the picture below.
2. On the whole, the entire grouping of elements fuse together to create a symmetrical design that resembles a star.
3. If we examine it more closely, we recognize the "whole" consists of several stars of varying scale: small, medium, and large. These individual stars are essential elements of the quilt block and contribute to its overall design.
4. If we study each star individually, we learn each is made of a series of geometric shapes: triangles, squares, and rectangles.
5. Further, depending on our perspective as we view the "whole," we start to see how each individual element contributes to the sym-

metrical structure of the design. We have gotten inside the structure of the complete design and understand how it works.

Thinking Skill #3: Creative Thinking

Analytical thinking is about taking something apart in order to understand how it works. Creative thinking is about putting parts together in new and useful ways. In script analysis, we call that new and useful way an "interpretation."

Some people are mystified, even intimidated, by the idea of being "creative." Why do we find creativity scary? For one thing, it's not entirely under conscious control. Creativity draws upon the unconscious, including such mysterious methods as intuition and insight. For another thing, we usually aren't encouraged to practice creativity; our educational system has emphasized conscious, logical thinking. Finally, some believe: "I can't be creative. You have to be born with a creativity gene, and I wasn't."

But what if, as many educators and scientists believe, all humans have the capacity to be creative? What if that capacity just needs to be nurtured and developed? Recently, some neuroscientists have argued that creative thinking is part of normal brain function; a lack of it could lead to depression and anxiety.

Furthermore, the better you understand creativity, the more you realize that the conscious and unconscious work as partners in this type of thinking. Those who have studied creativity tend to agree that there are multiple steps in the process:

1. Define the goal or problem clearly (conscious step). If you don't know what you need, you're not likely to find it.
2. Feed your mind (conscious step). Do research on the topic. The conscious mind needs information about the problem. The unconscious mind must be nourished by a different kind of meal. The unconscious has a taste for visual images, sounds, smells, flavors, movement, patterns and paradoxes. Even things that don't seem logically relevant can stimulate an idea in the unconscious.
3. Give your conscious mind a rest and let the unconscious go to work (unconscious step). This "rest" phase is important. At

a moment when you're not thinking about the problem at all, your unconsciousness may pop a creative solution into your mind. Eureka! Insight!

4. Evaluate and refine your idea (conscious step). If your testing of the idea reveals that it just won't work, then you may need to go back to step 2 — or even step 1.

Following this procedure doesn't guarantee that your unconscious will create something fabulous. However, not following the procedure guarantees that you won't create anything. You need conscious work to understand the puzzle and to give the unconscious the pieces to put together in new ways. You also need to allow plenty of time for the unconscious to shuffle the pieces until it comes up with a pattern that fits the puzzle.

What does the unconscious do to create new ideas? In his classic work, *The Act of Creation: A Study of the Conscious and Unconscious in Science and Art,* Arthur Koestler argues that the unconscious mind intuitively matches — in the form of **analogy** — structures or patterns originating from two fields of study, patterns that haven't been brought together before.

So if analogical thinking is an aspect of creative thinking, then what is an analogy? Holyoak and Thagard suggest that humans make analogies in an effort to use comparison to something familiar in order to understand something unfamiliar. For instance, if a very young child said, "My toes are the fingers of my feet," she would be doing analogical thinking. Note that an analogy has at least four parts and often compares *functions* or *relationships* between things. In this example, the child is saying, my toes (unfamiliar) are to my feet (unfamiliar) as my fingers (familiar) are to my hand (familiar). Both are small, moveable appendages that can pick up things. An analogy can also be expressed in the form of an algebraic equation:

$$A : B :: X : Y$$

$$\text{Toes: feet :: fingers : hands}$$

We use analogic thinking to construct, gradually, our mental model of the world. As the child grows older, she doesn't need to compare her toes to her fingers anymore; that comparison has been integrated into the world view, or *paradigm,* she carries in her mind. However, our mental models of the world are never complete maps of "reality," and false analogies may get built into them. People often stubbornly cling to their mental models, resisting creative ideas that challenge those maps.

Analogies usually compare things from two different "domains," or areas of life. If Pete's dad praises him for the birthday gift he chose for Uncle Mack by saying, "You hit a home run there, son," the dad is drawing an analogy between success in the field of baseball and success in the area of family relationships.

Creative ideas often appear in the form of unexpected analogies that emerge from the correspondence between two domains. In a famous story about scientific creativity, the chemist Kekulé reported dozing off and dreaming about rows of molecules which twisted like snakes, until one of the snakes bit its tail. This image drawing analogies from chemistry and nature inspired Kekulé's prediction that the benzene molecule is circular in structure, like the snake swallowing its tail.

Another way of envisioning creativity is as a blend of **convergent** and **divergent** thinking. Convergent thinking uses logic, research, and other traditional methods to solve a problem for which there is usually one right answer. Divergent thinking means generating lots of potential solutions (as in "brainstorming") for an open-ended problem which may have a number of possible answers. In the steps given above, divergent thinking could enter the process during step 2 and/or step 3. Steps 1 and 4 are largely convergent, though sometimes a new way of seeing the problem helps.

EXERCISE 1:2
Which descriptions fit me?

As we identify some of the characteristics of a creative thinker, think about whether you recognize yourself in each description. Put an X beside each characteristic you see in yourself.

___ Creative thinkers are flexible thinkers. They can think about ideas from many perspectives. They can see an idea from the "bird's eye view" or from the "worm's eye view."

___ Creative thinkers are motivated intrinsically rather than extrinsically. They work on a task because they have a passion for it

___ Creative thinkers welcome constructive critique. They seek feedback, knowing that they can always improve.

___ Creative thinkers are open to innovation manifesting itself through emotions, intuitions, images, and physical feelings. They understand that great ideas may arise from unlikely places at unexpected times.

___ Creative thinkers recognize that creative thinking is nurtured by experience and deep reflection on experience. It does not spring forth from a vacuum.

___ Creative thinkers develop a set of thinking tools that facilitate creativity, including the ability to recognize and form patterns; think abstractly; communicate ideas through metaphors, analogies and images; and empathize.

___ Creative thinkers take risks. They are open to considering alternatives that may be perceived by others as "crazy." They push boundaries: their own and their societies'.

Risk-taking is crucial for creativity. Humanistic psychologist Rollo May wrote a book called *The Courage to Create*. If you can master the fear of looking foolish or being "wrong," you are well on your way to creative adventures. If you would like to explore creative thinking, try out the exercises below.

EXERCISE 1:3
Visual
creativity

1. Look again at the quilt block in Example 1:2
2. Is there another way to create a quilt block that is symmetrical and made up of stars? Take out paper and pencil and doodle around with the stars.
3. How about an asymmetrical interpretation?
4. Now take a look at the list of geometric shapes that make up the stars.
5. Are there other ways to combine the triangles, squares, and rectangles into stars? Doodle around with the geometric shapes and see what other "star-like" figures you can make.
6. Take your new stars and put them into a symmetrical or asymmetrical quilt block.

EXERCISE 1:4
The "magic if"

Let's practice a different kind of creative thinking, a kind actors use.

Stanislavski, founder of modern acting theory, proposed a valuable tool for actors: the **Magic If**. Stanislavski wanted the actor to "believe" in the character and the world of the play. If the actor didn't believe, neither would the audience. But an actor mustn't try to convince himself, "I am Hamlet." That way lies insanity. Instead, the actor says to himself, "*If* I were Hamlet and in Hamlet's situation, how would I feel? What would I do?" The Magic If provides the bridge between actor and character; it allows for **empathy**; it helps the actor get caught up in the play's action. Another version, "*What if …* ?" can spur creativity too.

What if the "*Magic If*" could help you learn script analysis? Consider the following character:

Character A is a student taking this class. Character A passionately wants a career as a theatrical artist. Script analysis is an essential skill for all theatrical artists whether they be performers, directors, or designers. Character A sees that the depth and thoroughness of his analysis will serve as the springboard for creative performance and design choices; he knows artists must take risks, plunging into the unknown without fear of making mistakes.

Now use the "Magic If." Ask yourself, "*if* I were Character A, how would I feel? What would I do?" As Character A,

1. Write a list of things you believe would help you learn script-analysis.
2. Write a second list of obstacles you think might get in the way.
3. Make a third list of things you can do to overcome those obstacles.
4. Share your lists with a partner.

Keep these lists in your portfolio. Make a commitment to yourself that for the duration of this class you will act *as if* you want to be a professional performer, director, designer, playwright, or reviewer — all of whom must learn script analysis. Each time, before you start working on a new assignment, review the lists.

If you don't think of yourself as a creative thinker yet, you have come to the right place! Script analysis will give you the opportunity to discover and develop each of the creative characteristics we listed. By the time you finish this course you will be well acquainted with analytical and creative thinking. But there is still one more kind of thinking that you need to be an intellectual "triple threat": **critical thinking**. Critical thinking will enable you to assess your ideas and make sure you've understood each of the script analysis tools. Critical thinking will help you decide which interpretation of the script best represents the meaning you want to communicate to your audience.

Thinking Skill #4: Critical Thinking; or, "How Do I Know When I Have the 'Right' Answer?"

Critical thinking requires us to venture beyond unexamined personal preference or bias. Just as we inherit the color of our eyes we also inherit biases about all kinds of issues from the adults that raise us. Critical thinking gives us the ability to examine our received biases and decide for ourselves what we believe. Critical thinking is necessary in order to address questions *for which one absolute, true-with-a-capital-T answer cannot be found.* Most questions of significance are that type of question. Critical thinking involves a number of steps and demands a number of skills:

From a study of college students at Harvard (1970), William Perry formulated a theory about developmental stages in students' critical thinking. Critical thinking, he proposed, relates strongly to a student's worldview. Building upon Perry and others, Craig Nelson describes four stages in the development of critical thinking. We have changed each stage's title while keeping Nelson's four stages.

- **Colonel Quaritch (Worldview: Dualism)** This character from *Avatar* provides the metaphor for a worldview in which all questions, whether intellectual or moral — have a "right" and "wrong" answer. Authority knows all the "right" answers; teachers are authorities; thus teachers are expected to give students the "right" answers. Take another look at the scene in which the Colonel, inciting his troops to attack the Na'vi, keeps telling them everything he wants them to believe "is a fact."

- **"Whatever!" (Worldview: Multiplicity)** Once the snake of uncertainty slithers into this academic Garden of Eden, students undergo a pendulum swing into *Whatever!* If nothing is absolutely true, then everyone's opinion must be as good as everyone else's (except for those certainties on which all authorities still agree). I can change what you wrote on Wikipedia, for instance, and somebody else can change what I wrote.

It doesn't matter whether any of the three of us actually know what we're talking about. If somebody posted something on the Internet, that something has to be true. Studies show the majority of graduating college seniors use the *Whatever!* mode of thinking about issues in the real world.

- **Basketball vs. Quidditch (Worldview: Contextual Relativism).** The third stage arises when the student realizes that although there may not be eternally true answers to all questions, some solutions are better than others. Different cultures, different sports, different subject fields have different rules and standards. Different situations call for different responses. The issue then, becomes: on what grounds, or according to what *criteria*, does one evaluate the various alternatives? At this point, the student has to find out what standards the disciplinary field she is studying applies to the task at hand — and use those criteria to evaluate her own work. *It is in this stage that a student actually begins to engage in critical thinking.*

- **Choosing your own golden snitch.** The fourth stage **(Worldview: Commitment),** requires a person to accept relativity and uncertainty but still take responsibility for his actions. This individual compares the methods and values of different disciplines and chooses among them. Self-aware, she commits herself to acting according to her own values, although that commitment means making difficult choices without being sure of the consequence. This worldview balances the flexibility needed in a rapidly changing environment with the sense of being centered in one's own identity.

Read each of the four stages carefully. Write your responses to each of the questions below, then share your answers with a partner or small group.

EXERCISE 1:5
Which stage?

1. Which of the four stages best describes how you think most of the time? Why do you think the way you do? Can you identify any assumptions underlying the way you think?

2. Which stage best describes how you think about science. Why do you think the way you do? Can you identify any assumptions underlying the way you think about science?

3. Which stage best describes how you think about English literature? Why do you think the way you do? Can you identify any assumptions underlying the way you think about English literature?

4. Which stage best describes how you think about politics? Why do you think the way you do? Can you identify any assumptions underlying the way you think about politics?

Perry's classification scheme isn't absolute. For one thing, an individual may be Colonel Quaritch in some areas of knowledge and "Whatever!" in another. He might also swing back and forth among the modes depending on the weather. We should remember too that the Perry theory is itself not an absolute but founded upon a particular worldview based on the belief that knowledge is constructed.

In order to perform script analysis effectively, you need to engage in the level of critical thinking we call Basketball vs. Quidditch. In other words, you have to learn the criteria the discipline of Theatre uses for evaluating the results of your application of each of the script analysis tools. You then use those standards to help you revise your analysis.

What are criteria and how do I use them?

A criterion is a standard, test, or rule for evaluating the *quality* or *validity* of something. When we talked about "standards" in the section on mental management, we could have chosen the world **criteria**. We may forget that we actively engage in critical thinking — with criteria — every day to help us make all kinds of choices from what kind of bread to buy to who to vote for in an election. Unless we are **mindful** of it, we may not realize how much we use criteria in our decision making.

For example, use the "Magic If" and imagine that you're a basketball coach at Bop University. You're holding try-outs for your team. What might be some of the criteria you use to evaluate the athletes who try out?

Some criteria may be hard and fast rules. Probably one criterion (rule) is that all members of the Bop University basketball team must be students enrolled at Bop University. So, Coach, you can't just go out and hire a pro basketball player to play on your team. You must make sure that everyone you choose is a currently enrolled Bop U student.

Other criteria may be more flexible but related to the game of basketball. For instance, good basketball players tend to be tall so that they can reach the basket easily. Height, then, is usually a criterion for evaluating potential players.

An athlete's ability to make baskets and shoot free-throws is another criterion for making the team. Indeed, any ability or skill that helps a person to play the game well is a criterion. What are some of the other criteria that you as Coach need to consider?

A good basketball coach will know what skills to look for in picking a team. If you don't know the criteria the game of basketball requires of its players, you won't be a good coach. You won't know what kind of people you need to create a winning team.

Different activities require different criteria. Height, for instance, which is a criterion for a good basketball center, is not necessary for a poker player, whereas the ability to keep a straight face while holding all four aces might be a criterion for the card shark.

1. Make a list of the criteria needed for
   - an excellent student
   - the President of the United States
   - an outstanding musician
2. Compare lists with a classmate.

EXERCISE 1:6
Creating criteria

1. Make a list of the criteria you would consider when …
   - choosing which film to go see tonight?
   - choosing which car to buy?
   - choosing your college major?
2. Compare lists with a classmate.
3. Now consider what information you would need about the film, car, and major in order to decide which choice best meets your criteria.
4. Where might you find that information?
5. How would you evaluate each source of information? What criteria would you use?

EXERCISE 1:7
Using criteria

Criteria vary according to the task to be accomplished and the field of study, but they are always present when we are thinking critically whether we are aware of them or not. Each script analysis task has a set of criteria, which you need to use to evaluate your analysis. Criteria are a major key to critical thinking. If you learn how to use criteria in this course, you should be able to transfer your critical thinking skills to other fields of study. You just need to ask: What are the criteria?

How do all these types of thinking work with each other?

Thinking is a complex activity by nature: messy, ambiguous, and sometimes uncomfortable. In this chapter, we presented analytical, creative, and critical thinking as if their relationship to one another were consecutive when, often, it is concurrent. Information derived from analytical thinking may need some critical attention before it moves on to nourishing creativity. Creative expression may need some "tweaking" through analysis and then be subjected to critical thinking. Critical thinking may stimulate creative expression and uncover places where further analysis could enhance the final product. The point is, each type of thinking is influenced by the other two and all three are engaged in an intricate looping dance with first one in the lead then another. If you keep this in mind as you learn each tool of script analysis, you will see how the tools relate to each other and the final product: an interpretation of a script that can bring to life on the stage a significant understanding of human experience.

Why do I need to do so much writing?

*Writing **is** thinking.* Writing is not just a way to communicate ideas *after* they have formed. It's a way to *get* ideas and develop them. As we suggested, the different kinds of thinking work together, hand in hand. If we don't write our ideas down, we can't see how one idea could affect our understanding of another idea. Furthermore, by writing things down, we can improve our thinking. We can check our ideas by applying the criteria for that analytical tool. We can polish and refine our ideas through the process of revision until the ideas we want to communicate shine through clearly.

Theatre artists find joy in creativity. Script analysis involves creative thinking and can generate the same kind of joy in discovery: Aha! Now I get it!

1. Reread the thought you wrote down at the beginning of this chapter.
2. Has your thought changed after reading the chapter?
3. Whether or not your ideas about thinking tools have changed, you have just paid attention to your thinking instead of taking it for granted.

EXERCISE 1:8
Mental management

Chapter 2
Given Circumstances

What are "given circumstances?"

Given Circumstances (GC) is a theatrical term for the physical and psychological environment in which a story takes place. GC provide answers to basic questions about who, what, where, and when. **Constantine Stanislavski** (1863-1938) first introduced the idea of given circumstances as a way of grounding the actor's imaginative work in the specific context of a particular story. To understand the context in which events take place, we first identify each GC individually

Analysis of GC requires us to find and categorize pieces of information. First we take the script apart, making sure not to miss significant circumstances, and then synthesize the pieces into a full summary of the **world of the play**. We will be relying on our ability to think analytically and critically in this chapter. Information revealed by the given circumstances will later nurture our creative thinking as we move towards articulating an interpretation.

How are given circumstances used in the production process?

Given circumstances lay the groundwork for the whole process. We could say that GC "seed" the production process with essential nutrients. All the members of the artistic team use GC to feed and guide their thinking. GC influence the actors' understanding of who they are portraying, the designers' understanding of where and when the story takes place and the director's vision of what the script is about. They provide the artistic team with a common touchstone in team discussions. Clear communication amongst the team is essential for the process to result in a unified interpretation.

What kind of information qualifies as a given circumstance?

GC provide information about *who, what, where,* and *when* in the story. By answering the questions below, you can identify the given circumstances in a script.

1. **Who** are the characters and what kinds of relationships do they share with each other?
   a. Are family units represented among the characters and if so what are those familial relationships?
   b. Are there lovers among the characters?
   c. Which characters are friends or acquaintances?
   d. Which characters are hostile towards one another?
   e. Are there changes in any relationships in the course of the script?
2. **What** social institutions and groups govern the world of the play?
   a. What vocational groups are represented?
   b. What social classes are represented?
   c. What political system circumscribes the lives of the characters?
   d. What economic system motivates and constrains behavior?
   e. Are there any references to characters' ethical, religious, or spiritual beliefs?
3. **Where** does the story take place?
   a. Can you identify the national, regional, and local sites in which the story takes place?
   b. Are there interior and/or exterior locations?
   c. Do specific architectural or topographical features define the space?
   d. Are specific sites such as a jail or a bedroom or a board room required for the action of the story?
4. **When** does the story take place?
   a. What are the day, date, month, and year for each scene?
   b. How much time passes before the story is completed?
   c. Is time used in any special way? Accelerated? Decelerated? Paused?

Just like a character in a story, you have given circumstances that frame your world. Understanding your circumstances and how you interact with them clarifies the reasoning behind the decisions you make. Try the exercise below to gain a better understanding of how a change in circumstance can dictate a change in outcome.

EXERCISE 2:1
Finding your personal given circumstances

1. Go through the questions listed above. Answer each one as if you were a character.
2. Identify one long-range objective you have for yourself such as, "get a college degree," or "marry the person I love" or "have a large family," or "have a successful career."

GC are not static over the course of a lifetime. GC are dynamic. As one old adage says, "Nothing is more certain in life than change." A change in a circumstance can change how we pursue objectives and determine what choices are possible.

EXERCISE 2:2
The dynamic nature of given circumstances

1. Stop and think for a moment about how different your journey towards your objective would be if:
   a. you lived in the year 1776 or 1917 or 1942.
   b. you won $100,000.00 in a lottery
   c. you were a citizen of China, or Iran, or North Korea
2. Choose a major change in your personal circumstances. Speculate on how the change might affect your ability to accomplish the goal you chose in Exercise 2:1.

Characters in a script, just like real people, are shaped by the particular world in which they live. If we discover the script's given circumstances we get closer to understanding why characters do what they do. Figuring out character motivation provides clues to the script's meaning, which takes us one step closer to our eventual goal: forming an interpretation that provides insight into some aspect of human nature.

How do I recognize a given circumstance in a script?

Now that we know what questions to ask we need to know how to recognize the answer. Playwrights often don't reveal given circumstances overtly. Sometimes we need to integrate pieces of information scattered through several lines of dialogue and **stage directions**. For instance, in the opening lines from George Bernard Shaw's *Arms and the Man,* several bits of information help us identify the time of day without the specific time being mentioned. As we work through the lines below, notice the words in bold type and italics: clues to the time of day during which the opening scene takes place.

> Catherine [*Entering hastily, full of good news*] Raina! [*She pronounces it Rah-eena, with the stress on the ee*] Raina! [*She goes to the **bed**, expecting to find Raina there*] Why, where — ? [*Raina looks into the room*]. Heavens child! Are you out in the **night air** instead of in your **bed**? You'll catch your death. Louka told me you were **asleep**.
>
> Raina [*Dreamily*] I sent her away. I wanted to be alone. The **stars** are beautiful! What is the matter?

Four clues in the dialogue point to the time of day: **night air, bed, asleep,** and **stars.** Stage directions which reference *bed* and characterize Raina's delivery as *dreamily* provide supporting evidence. With some measure of certainty we can say it is night time as the script opens, perhaps late at night given Catherine's reaction to Raina still being awake.

Additionally, the same line, or even the same word, may contain clues to more than one type of circumstance. "Bed" not only starts us thinking about *when* the scene is happening, it also starts to define *where* the scene may be taking place. The preceding lines also contain clues about the time of year, the type of relationship between the two characters, the nature of the relationship with an offstage third character, and spiritual beliefs of at least one character. Can you identify the clues? Of course, you need to read the whole script carefully to verify or challenge these initial observations.

A word is needed here to clarify the nature of stage directions: be sure you find out who authored them. The playwright may have written them for the purpose of clarifying circumstances and relationships. The stage manager or director of a previous production might have added them, in which case they reflect that production's interpretation of the script. Stage directions, especially those authored by the playwright, can be useful in confirming what the dialogue reveals but they are not more valid than the clues in the dialogue.

You might want to know more about the whole story of *Arms and the Man,* from which we drew our GC example, so before you do the next exercise, we give you a synopsis of the script:

Arms and the Man (1894), is subtitled "An anti-romantic comedy." Shaw, a social critic, delighted in attacking what he saw as false social ideals. He divided people into three categories: the Idealist, the Realist, and the Philistine. The Philistines, the majority, accept social rules unquestioningly — smugly ignorant. The Idealists, a much smaller group, cause trouble because they think things *should* be better and try to achieve false ideals. The Realists (not many around) see the world as it "really" is.

In *Arms and the Man*, Shaw attacks romantic ideals about love and war. The script draws on an old folk tale. The Bulgarians are at war with the Serbs. A cavalry charge by the Serbs has routed the Bulgarians A Swiss soldier, Bluntschli, takes refuge in the bedroom of Raina, a Bulgarian maiden, who hides him from his pursuers. Raina, a romantic, is engaged to another romatic, Sergius, who led the cavalry charge. Raina becomes outraged when the anti-romantic Bluntschli, not knowing of Raina's engagement, calls the man who led the cavalry charge a fool. She also looks down on Bluntschli for his unsoldierly fear of being shot — and his love of chocolate creams. Nonetheless, she tells her mother about Bluntschli, and the two conspire to keep him hidden and send him off the next day in an old coat belonging to Raina's father.

Act II takes place in Raina's garden, after the end of the war. Sergius and Petkoff, Raina's father, return home. Sergius courts Raina romantically, with "the higher love," but makes passes behind her back at Louka, the serving-maid (who is engaged to the man servant Nicola). Sergius and Petkoff talk about meeting a Swiss soldier and hearing a funny tale about how he was saved after the battle by two Bulgarian women. Bluntschli arrives to return the coat and is invited to stay to lunch by Sergius and Petkoff.

In Act III, Bluntschli unmasks Raina, and she confesses that her romantic façade is indeed a pose. Louka reveals to Sergius that Bluntschli had spent the night after the battle in Raina's bedroom. Sergius challenges Bluntschli to a duel. In trying to extricate himself from this mess, Bluntschli confesses his attraction to Raina and castigates himself for being such a romantic fool. Since everyone has believed Bluntschli to be the plain-spoken, common-sense, feet-on-the-ground realist he had appeared to be, all are astounded. Louka ends up with Sergius, and Raina finally agrees to marry Bluntschli, who appeals to her as his vulnerable self, her "chocolate cream soldier."

1. Analyze the following scene for clues to its given circumstances. Look for clues that answer the basic questions of **who, what, where,** and **when.**
2. Create a system for recording the clues you find. Some people use color coding and highlight each type of clue with a different color. Some people write the name of each type of circumstance at the top of a document and "sift" the clues into the appropriate document like a series of buckets. The important thing is that you work with a system that facilitates your understanding of the clues. The sifted and recorded clues are your evidence for the conclusions you will report.
3. Report your conclusions in an essay. Be sure to cover all four major types of given circumstances. If you conclude there are no clues to support a conclusion about a type of circumstance, say so in the essay. If you need graphs, tables, illustrations or other visual material to make your point(s) more clearly, feel free to include them.
4. Look at the given circumstances you have identified. Weave them together and describe the context in which the characters live during this scene.

Louka   There's a gentleman just called madam. A Serbian officer.

Catherine [*Flaming*] A Serb! And how dare he — [*Checking herself bitterly*] Oh, I forgot. We are at peace now. I suppose we shall have them calling every day to pay their compliments. Well: if he is an officer why don't you tell your master? He is in the library with Major Saranoff. Why do you come to me?

Louka   But he asks for you madam. And I don't think he knows who you are: he said the lady of the house. He gave me this ticket for you. [*She takes a card out of her bosom; puts it on a salver tray; and offers it to Catherine.*]

Catherine [*Reading*] "Captain Bluntschili?" That's a German name.

Louka   Swiss, Madam, I think.

Catherine [*With a bound that makes Louka jump back*] Swiss! What is he like?

Louka   [*Timidly*] He has a big carpet bag, Madam

Catherine Oh Heavens! He's come to return the coat. Send him away: say we're not at home; ask him to leave his address and I'll write him. Oh stop: that will never do. Wait! [*She throws herself into a chair to think about it*] The Master and Major Saranoff are busy in the library aren't they?

Louka   Yes, Madam.

Catherine [*Decisively*] Bring the gentleman out here at once. [*Peremptorily*] And be very polite to him. Don't delay. Here [*Impatiently snatching the salver from her*]: leave that here; and go straight back to him.

Louka   Yes. Madam [*Going*]

Catherine Louka!

Louka   [*Stopping*] Yes, Madam.

Catherine Is the library door shut?

Louka   I think so, Madam.

Catherine If not, shut it as you pass through.

Louka   Yes, Madam [*Going*]

Catherine Stop! [*Louka stops*] He will have to go that way. [*Indicating the gate into the stableyard*] Tell Nicola to bring his bag here after him. Don't forget.

Louka   [*Surprised*] His bag?

Catherine Yes: here: as soon as possible. [*Vehemently*] Be quick!

How do given circumstances interact with other tools of script analysis?

Playwrights carefully structure the action in scripts in order to create a rising tide of tension, curiosity, and suspense in the audience. Changes in a character's real or perceived given circumstances heighten the dramatic tension and drive the dramatic action forward. When you see a place in a script where a circumstance changes or is first revealed you often find a major structural building block.

GC do more than help structure action; they also help explain why characters behave the way they do and what kind of people they are in their "heart of hearts." Characters choose objectives to pursue and tactics for achieving their objectives based on their core identity. Playwrights place characters into circumstances that will both reveal and challenge a character's core identity, pushing a character into a moral crisis.

Example 2:1 Given Circumstances and Character Development

As an example, let's look at how given circumstances have shaped the character of Jake Sully, the protagonist in the film *Avatar*.

Jake Sully is a protagonist who is broken physically and spiritually. Physically, he has lost the use of his legs. Spiritually, he is broken by the death of his brother. Note that Jake has lost more than a sibling; it is his *twin*, a genetic reiteration of himself. That particular given circumstance deepens the wound and provides the circumstance through which Jake enters the Na'vi world. Both his physical and spiritual wounds cause him to question his identity and self-worth.

Other circumstances supporting his core identity as "a broken man" appear in the external environment. Jake is a soldier. The story is set in a war zone. Wars break things: people, cultures, villages, ecosystems, etc. The particular war in which Jake is engaged has broken a planet into two worlds: the mechanistic world of the corporate colony and the natural world of the Na'vi. This divided environment is an external reflection of the war raging inside Jake.

It is obvious in Jake's relationships with his peers and superiors that his broken body is considered a liability. Even the scientists who hope to reconcile with the Na'vi consider Jake inferior, a "moron." He no longer fits into the world of war as an able-bodied soldier and he does not fit into the scientific world of his twin whom he has replaced. Jake will have to redefine who he thinks he is.

For Jake, the desire to fix what is broken in him drives his actions. It is no coincidence that he has a spinal injury. The author may have chosen this particular given circumstance as an external reflection of Jake's inner disability. A healthy spine is central to our ability to move through the world with ease and efficiency. Parts of it literally rest in the center of our bodies. Jake's broken spine is a literal manifestation of the break in his core self-image.

Jake's original objective is to repair his physical spine, but a change in circumstances triggers Jake's realization that he is broken on the inside as well. From this point forward, his actions change because what he wants changes.

Collectively, the given circumstances of a story weave a contextual web that supports the issues the playwright is exploring and points the theatrical artist towards an interpretation. Within the script's circumstances are embedded visual and aural imagery that highlight the thematic threads. Looking at *Avatar* in relation to the given circumstance of *where*, we cannot avoid the stark circumstantial contrast between the natural, harmonious world of the Na'vi and the mechanized and discordant world of the corporate colonizers. What themes do these two locales suggest to us? While we are noticing circumstances, does it make a difference that the colonizers are corporate rather than governmental? The given circumstances echo through every aspect of the script analysis process. They provide its foundation.

Given circumstances, in collaboration with other script analysis tools inspire a unified interpretation called a Central Production Metaphor, which we will describe in chapter 8. You learn the uses of each tool individually but, on the job, theatrical artists alternate tools to generate varying insights which will eventually coalesce in a unified vision.

What Are the Criteria for Given Circumstances?

So far in this chapter, you have been using your analytical abilities: taking something apart in order to understand how it works. Using criteria to evaluate your findings will give your critical thinking a workout. Compare your ideas to the standards, or criteria, established for each task. Below are criteria for assessing the accuracy and completeness of your analysis of GC in a script.

- Choices should accurately reflect what is actually in the script rather than assumptions or inventions. Creativity comes later.
- The analysis must be based on a careful reading of the script, and justified with evidence. If you haven't read the script closely

several times, you've likely missed important information.
- Inferences made from a series of references in the script should be logical and consistent
- The analysis should be complete and answer the *who, what, where, when* of the story
- There should be an accurate summary of the cultural context into which the story is embedded based on a synthesis of all the given circumstances.

Capstone Assignment: Given Circumstances

Part A: Analysis

1. Read a full-length script chosen by your instructor.
2. Analyze it for given circumstances. Be sure to include all four types.
3. Report your conclusions in an essay. If you need graphs, tables, illustrations or other kinds of visual material to make your point(s) more clearly, feel free to include them. Include a summary of the world in which the story "lives." Think of describing a foreign country you have just visited to a friend.
4. Use the Peer Review Checklist in Appendix B to get feedback from a friend or classmate.
5. Revise your essay where you feel the peer feedback will strengthen and clarify your ideas.

Part B: Mental Management: Reflection

1. Describe the system you created for recording and organizing the given circumstances you identified in this assignment. Why does this system work well for you?
   or
2. If you did Exercise 2:3, did you change your system for this assignment? Why? Compare the two methods you used and talk about why one works better for you than the other.

Peer Review Checklists for each Capstone Assignment can be found in Appendix B.

Chapter 3
Action and Structural Analysis

What is the structure of action in a script?

"Lights, Camera, ACTION!"

Understanding ACTION is the key to script analysis. Aristotle (384-32 B.C.), the first dramatic theorist, named action the most important element in drama. A play, said Aristotle, is an imitation of an action *in the form of action*. What a character *does* means more than what she *says*.

The *actions* of characters create the structure of the script. If a script were a building, actions would provide the structural beams and girders that keep it aloft. If a script were a body, all the actions attached to each other would form the skeleton. To understand how a script is organized, we need to discover the significant actions and how they relate to one another. The ebb and flow of actions create moments of tension and release which keep an audience glued to their seats.

Seeing dramatic structure visually portrayed gives us a starting point for analysis. One famous diagram is called Freytag's Pyramid. It looks like this:

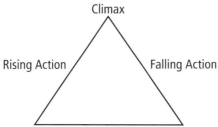

Figure 3:1
Freytag's Pyramid

Freytag based his model on the gradual rise of audience tension and suspense to a climax; from that peak, tension slowly diminishes until the script's end. The diagram devotes equal amounts of time to rising and falling action. Freytag's pyramid places the climax near the middle of the script. In production, however, a mid-play climax leaves the second half anti-climactic, thus boring.

We suggest an organizational model more useful for practicing theatre artists. Our visual representation of a script's structure looks like this:

Figure 3:2
Diagram of
script structure

So what do we mean when we talk about **action** in a script? What is an action? An action is something someone *does*. So if I scratch my nose, is that an action? Not in in script analysis terms. Scratching my nose is an **activity**, an insignificant "doing" that doesn't require thought on my part. An action in a script is significant and conscious. A character *wants* something. That desire stimulates the character to take conscious action to fulfill it. In order to understand an action in a script, we need to figure out: *why* is the character taking this action? *what* does he want? *how much* does he want it? *What is he willing to do* to get it?

What is the pattern of actions in a script?

Triggers and Heaps

In daily life, we may not know how one person's action relates to the action of somebody else. In a script, however, characters' actions are carefully put together to form a meaningful structure like links in a chain pulling the story forward. A script can be analyzed as a pattern of actions, a sequence of causes and effects. David Ball, in *Backwards and Forwards*, sees actions in scripts as linked pairs, the first causing the second. Ball chooses the terms **trigger** and **heap**, based on a shooting metaphor: One character pulls the trigger on his gun. As a result, the other character falls in a heap.

In life, humans want to find out the cause of significant events in order to predict their occurrence and thus control what happens. A script dramatizes a story which may help audiences recognize important cause-effect patterns in real life.

In scripts, usually both trigger and heap are human actions. For instance, in "Sleeping Beauty," the Prince kisses Beauty (causal action/trigger), which wakes Beauty from her long sleep (effect/ heap). These cause/effect sequences move the story forward. When an audience watches a play, they don't know what effect an event will cause. Not knowing generates suspense. However, in order for a script to transition from page to stage, theatre artists must recognize and carefully stage the trigger/heap sequences.

We can't identify triggers and heaps the first time we read a script. We don't know what will happen next. Ball suggests that we read the script again — backwards. We find an effect first and then look for the action which caused it. Starting at the script's end, we gradually work our way through the pattern of actions, from heap to trigger.

Where Does Conflict Fit into the Pattern?

Scripts are also based on actions, internal or external, that cause **conflict**. The three basic types of conflict are:

- Person vs. person (one person in conflict with another)
- Person vs. self (inner conflict)
- Person vs. forces larger than him/herself (God, Nature, Fate, Society, etc.)

A script may include all three types of conflict. We may claim we want to live "happily ever after," but onstage a play with no conflict is boring.

Who's Who in a Conflict?

The main character in a script is called the **protagonist.** The protagonist isn't necessarily the "good guy." *Macbeth*, for instance, features a murderer as protagonist. *Star Wars* I, II, and III tell the story of Anakin Skywalker, aka Darth Vader. To identify the script's protagonist, ask yourself: Whose story is it? Protagonists often go through a process of change, so you can also ask: Who changes the most?

Because scripts contain conflict, characters and forces push against one another, each trying to get what he/she wants. An **antagonist** is a character who opposes the protagonist. At a very elemental level, a play is like a sporting event: Who will win? A football or basketball game in which the lead shifts back and forth generates more suspense and excitement than one in which it's obvious who will triumph. As we analyze the triggers and heaps, we also trace the conflict. Does a particular trigger help or hinder the protagonist in his/her struggle?

EXERCISE 3:1
Patterns of action in daily life

1. What are some cause-effect patterns you've noticed in daily life? Perhaps start with patterns in nature: What causes the sun to appear to "set"? What causes rain? What makes flowers close at night and open in the morning? In these cases, usually someone has observed an effect and then worked backwards to find out the cause.

2. Next think of patterns in which both cause and effect are human actions. For instance, what made your mother yell at you? Why did your best friend stop talking to you? What caused the teacher to frown at you when you asked a question? In these cases, you're still starting with the effect, but the cause may or may not be something you did.

3. Now think of patterns in which you really want to know what action you need to take to cause a desired effect: What would you have to do to get a student loan? What would you say to a classmate to get him/her to help you study for an exam? If you wanted the person you love to love you, what would you need to do?

4. Decide on a goal you strongly want to achieve. What action(s) would you take in order to cause that effect?

How Do Patterns of Actions and Conflict Go Together?

Most people would identify Cinderella as the main character of her tale. However, let's imagine that Cinderella's Prince is the protagonist. He falls in love with Cinderella at the ball and wants to marry her. When the clock strikes midnight, Cinderella runs away. The Prince pursues but doesn't find Cinderella. Instead, he finds one of her glass slippers on the staircase.

From the point of view of the Prince, the conflict is of the type "person vs. person." The Prince wants to marry Cinderella but antagonists get in the way. Some triggers the Prince encounters are obstacles, some assist him. For instance, Cinderella runs away (trigger); the Prince pursues her (heap). This trigger and heap form one sequence in our script's structure. Cinderella's running away (trigger) serves as an obstacle to the Prince's goal. The Prince's pursuit of Cinderella (heap), however, leads him to another trigger that assists him: he finds the slipper. The slipper trigger provides him with a way to locate Cinderella: the next heap shows the Prince searching for the woman whose foot fits the slipper.

Remember, in analyzing the structure of a script, we also need to consider *why* these particular characters behave as they do. Why does Cinderella run away at midnight? Why does the Prince announce he will marry the woman whose foot fits the slipper? And so on. A theatre artist must be like a psychologist, drawing upon his understanding of human behavior.

1. Select a fairy tale or other story you know well.
2. Who is the protagonist?
3. Who are the antagonists?
4. Which characters assist the protagonist?
5. Identify several cause/effect sequences in the story. Antagonists or allies perform the trigger; the protagonist's responding action is the heap.
6. Why does each character behave as he/she does in each sequence you've identified? Try to figure out what the characters want.

EXERCISE 3:2
Analyzing patterns of action and conflict in a fairytale

1. Does this pattern of action occur in daily life?
2. Think of a conflict in which you've recently taken part. You, of course, are the protagonist.
3. See if you can identify several trigger/heap sequences that occurred.
4. Ask yourself: What was the other person's intention?
5. Why did I respond as I did?
6. What did each of us want?

EXERCISE 3:3
Analyzing patterns of action and conflict in daily life

If you don't remember a conflict in which you've participated, try
to think of one you've observed. Or keep your eyes open for conflict that arises in your presence.

How Is Action Structured In a Script?

The cause/effect actions arising from conflict are structured
around larger patterns which form a script's major building blocks.
If we imagine the script as a building, we see that the drama rises
in stages from the basement to the top floor. Take another look at
the diagram in fig. 3.2. Below we explain the major structural elements, giving some examples from *Oedipus the King*.

Exposition

Clues playwrights give about what occurred before the story began, or offstage. Exposition gives the audience information they
need to understand what happens. Good playwrights weave the
exposition into the action, so each important revelation triggers
a complication.

Beginning Stasis

The Given Circumstances provide the information you need to
describe *the situation at the beginning of the script* before the main
action begins. Back-story, things major characters did in the past
that affect the main action, may also be part of the beginning
stasis. The beginning situation usually exists in uneasy balance.
There may be nasty secrets hidden in the "cellar." The inciting
incident will "tip the balance over" into action. In the opening
scene, exposition tells us some things about the stasis. Revelation
of other stasis information, however, may not happen until later.

The stasis of *Oedipus* includes the given circumstance that a
plague is devastating Thebes. Back-story: Oedipus, the protagonist, is king, having won the crown by answering the riddle of
the Sphinx and marrying Jocasta, the widow of the previous king,
Laius. Unknown to Oedipus, an oracle had told Laius that he
would die by the hand of his own child; therefore Laius sent his
newborn son away to be left to die on a mountainside. Unknown
to Jocasta, an oracle had told Oedipus he would kill his father and
marry his mother; therefore Oedipus left his home in Corinth to
escape fulfilling the prophesy. Prior to the opening of the play,

Oedipus has sent his brother-in-law Creon to ask the oracle what they can do to save the city.

Main Action

The most important action the protagonist tries to do throughout the script, expressed as a strong, active verb. The character *wants* to do this action, and his desire and will stimulate him to pursue the action for most of the story.

Inciting Incident

The significant trigger that sets the main action of the story (heap) in motion. It is a new piece of information or an action — some kind of problem — that upsets the beginning stasis. This event cannot have happened before the story begins; it *must occur onstage, during the story*. The inciting incident almost always stimulates the story's *protagonist* to take action, even though the full significance of that action may not become clear until later.

In *Oedipus*, Creon returns with the oracle's message that the plague has occurred to punish the city for harboring the murderer of Laius. Delivery of the oracle's message is the trigger of the inciting incident. Oedipus sets off on the main action of the script; he vows to find the murderer. Note that the plague itself cannot be the inciting incident because it was ravaging Thebes before the script began.

> **Protagonist's First Step:** The inciting incident triggers the main action of the story. The protagonist then chooses the first thing she will do to try to complete her main action. This first attempted solution of the problem posed by the inciting incident sets the protagonist on a path where he will bump into an obstacle — the trigger of the first major complication.

The first step Oedipus takes is to send for the blind prophet Tiresias, to interrogate him. When Tiresias arrives, Oedipus asks the prophet to tell all he knows about the murder of Laius.

Major Complication

Anything a character other than the protagonist does that affects which way the story's main action goes. A major complication is often an obstacle but it may also be unexpected help. **Complications** may arrive in the form of new information, opposition to a character's goals, or other actions of characters. A major complication is composed of a major trigger and heap.

Trigger: An event that causes a responding event, called a heap. The trigger is usually an action done by someone other than the protagonist.

Heap: An event that is a response to a preceding trigger, usually an action done by the protagonist in reaction to the trigger.

Obstacle: Anything that prevents the protagonist from completing his/her **main action**.

A complication usually interferes with the protagonist's achieving his/her goal. The protagonist cannot do what she set out to do, so she must adjust and choose another strategy. This *choice point* is called a **crisis**. The action the protagonist *chooses to take* as a result of the trigger is the complication's heap. When you analyze a script's structure, identify both the trigger and heap of each major complication.

The first major complication in *Oedipus the King* occurs in the scene between Oedipus and Tiresias. The prophet refuses to answer Oedipus's questions, and the two argue. Finally, Tiresias accuses Oedipus himself of being the murderer he seeks. In retaliation, Oedipus jumps to the conclusion that Tiresias and Creon are plotting to overthrow him, and he threatens the traitors.

To show how complications work, we now examine an important scene in which occurs the second major complication in *Oedipus the King* (in this translation, by Ruby Blondell, titled *King Oidipous*). Oedipus has just quarreled with Creon, accusing Creon of plotting with the blind prophet to blame Oedipus for the murder of Laius and thus steal the throne. Angry raised voices bring Queen Jocasta from the palace to find out what is going on. She questions her husband:

Jokasta   Tell me too, by the gods, my lord, the matter that
           has caused you to establish and retain such wrath.

Oidipous   I'll speak; for I revere you more than these folk, wife.
           It's Kreon, and the plans against me that he's hatched.

Jokasta   Speak clearly of the quarrel that you blame him for.

Oidipous   He says the murderer of Laios is myself.

Jokasta   He knows this for himself, or taught by someone else?

Oidipous   Neither. He sent an evil-working prophet here,
and so he keeps his own mouth fully free from blame.

Jokasta   Release yourself from fear about the matters that
you're speaking of. Listen to me and learn that there's
no mortal creature sharing in prophetic skill.
I shall reveal to you brief evidence of this:
An oracle once came to Laios — I won't say
from Phoibos, but from Phoibos' servants — saying that
his destiny would be to perish at the hand
of any child that would be born to him and me.
And yet, the story goes, some foreign robbers killed
him one day at a junction where three highways meet;
as for our child, three days had not passed since his birth
when Laios yoked his feet and had him thrown, at someone
else's hand, on the untrodden mountainside.
So Phoibos did not bring to pass that he should be
his father's murderer, or Laios suffer at
his own child's hand — the awful thing he feared; yet this
is what the words of prophecy marked out for them.
So pay them no attention; if a god seeks what
he needs, he'll easily uncover it himself.

Oidipous   What wandering of spirit, wife, has gripped me since
I heard you speak just now — what turbulence of thought!

Jokasta   What anxious thought arrests you and inspires these words?

Oidipous   Here's what I thought I heard you saying: Laios was
slaughtered right at a junction where three highways meet.

Jokasta   Yes — that is what was said, nor has the rumor ceased.

In the above section of the scene, Jocasta attempts to calm her husband by reassuring him that there is no truth in oracles. She confesses that a prophesy foretold that Laius would die at the hand of his own son, so Laius had the infant murdered. In the process of telling the story, however, Jocasta reveals that Laius was killed at a place "where three highways meet." Jocasta's revelation of where Laius died is the trigger of the second major complication. Now Oedipus is forced to confront the possibility that he may, in fact, have killed the king.

As Oedipus remembers killing an elderly man at a place where three roads meet, he experiences an intense emotional reaction. Oedipus and Jocasta both speak of the king's shock and fear. The text gives important cues to the actor about how to play Oedipus's response to his discovery that he may be the murderer. However, an emotional reaction cannot be the heap of the complication; the heap must be an action. Oedipus's discovery and the feelings the discovery evokes create the crisis of this complication — the choice point for the protagonist. What will Oedipus *do* as a result of his discovery? The scene continues:

Oidipous   Where is this spot at which he suffered such a thing?

Jokasta   The land's called Phocis, and the place is where the road
           forks, leading folk from Delphi and from Daulia.

Oidipous   And how much time has passed since the event occurred?

Jokasta   The city heard the proclamation just before
           you were revealed to us as ruler of this land.

Oidipous   Oh Zeus, what have you planned to do regarding me?

Jokasta   What is this, Oidipous, that so disturbs your heart?

Oidipous   Don't ask me yet; but tell me more of Laios — what
           was his physique, and was he still in manhood's prime?

Jokasta   His hair was dark, just blooming with a sheen of white;
           and in appearance he was not too far from you.

Oidipous   Alas, wretch that I am! It seems I have just cast
           an awful curse upon myself in ignorance.

Jokasta   What do you mean? I shudder as I gaze at you!

Oidipous   My heart fears awfully the prophet may have sight.
           Say one more thing, and you will point me to the truth.

Jokasta   I shudder, but I'll speak—when I learn what you ask.

Oidipous   Did he proceed with few attending him, or with
           the kind of retinue that suits a ruling man?

Jokasta   The group was five in number altogether, one
           a herald; and a single carriage carried Laios.

Oidipous   Aiai! These things are now transparent! Tell me, wife,
           who was the person who reported this to you?

Jokasta   The only one who got back safely: a house-slave.

Oidipous   Tell me, is he by chance still present in the house?

Jokasta   No longer. When he came back here and saw that you
            were holding power, and Laios dead, he touched my hand
            in supplication, begging me to send him to
            the countryside to pasture flocks, so that he might
            be out of sight of town as far as possible.
            I sent him; since he was deserving, for a slave,
            to win this favor or an even greater one.

Oidipous   Then how can he return here quickly, back to us?

In spite of the terrible probability that he has condemned himself
to exile for the murder of Laius, Oedipus chooses to pursue the
truth. He cross-examines Jocasta and ultimately sends for the servant, the only living witness to the killing. As the scene goes on,
Oedipus confesses to Jocasta that he himself killed someone who
might have been Laius at the place where three highways meet.
He hopes that the house-slave, now a herdsman, will stick to the
story that Laius was killed by a band of robbers, since Oedipus
traveled alone. Oedipus's action of summoning the herdsman in
his pursuit of truth is the heap of the major complication:

Oidipous   You said he spoke of men who killed him, robbers in
            the plural; if that's still the number that he says,
            I'm not the killer: many cannot equal one.
            But if he clearly mentions one man traveling
            alone, the balance of the deed then tilts my way.

Jokasta   Know well this is the way his story was revealed;
            it is impossible that he disown it now,
            since all the city heard these things, not me alone.
            But even if he deviates from what he said
            back then, never will he reveal that it is true,
            my lord, that Laios' murder was predicted right,
            for Loxias expressly said that he must die
            at my son's hands; yet it was never my unhappy
            child that killed him, since the infant perished first.
            Therefore, as far as prophecy's concerned, I would
            in future not look this way as opposed to that.

Oidipous   You reason well. But all the same, send somebody
            to bring the laborer — do not omit this task.

Jokasta   I'll do it fast; but let's go back inside the house.
            I'd not do anything that was not dear to you.

Before the witness can appear, a messenger from Corinth arrives bringing Oedipus notice of his father's death and asking him to take his father's throne. Oedipus refuses to return to Corinth because an oracle once told him he would kill his father and marry his mother. In trying to encourage Oedipus to come home, the messenger informs Oedipus he was not the Corinthian king's real son but was adopted as a baby, thus triggering the third major complication. In spite of warnings from Jocasta that he shouldn't try to discover his real identity, Oedipus persists in his search for truth: he sends for the shepherd who gave him as an infant to the Corinthian messenger.

Note that the choice made at each crisis determines which way the protagonist's action goes: What will the character do now that she's blocked from the path she planned? The choice made usually leads to the next major complication. Furthermore, the nature of the choice made tells us a great deal about the character. Oedipus, for instance, could have chosen to hide the very possibility that he might have killed Laius. Like some politicians, he could have engaged in a cover-up to protect himself and retain his power.

Major complications are important building blocks in the script's structure, but since one leads to another, they're also links in a causal chain. Because they take the protagonist to unexpected places, complications contribute to audience engagement and suspense. They may also cause a change in the major dramatic question.

Major Dramatic Question What will happen at the end of the play? This question first arises in the audience's mind at the inciting incident. It changes as the story develops, usually becoming more meaningful.

Major crisis

The turning point when the protagonist must make a choice that determines the ending of the story is the major crisis. The crisis is caused by the most significant complication (trigger). The

Beginning Stasis: Bobby Boat's got treasure on his mind.

Inciting Incident: Bobby finds a map. It says he just has to cross The Uncharted Sea. X marks the spot! Smooth sailing ahead!

Complication #1: Trigger: Oh, no! A rocky cliff! That's not on the map. Bobby's not sure which way to go.

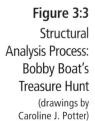

Figure 3:3
Structural Analysis Process: Bobby Boat's Treasure Hunt
(drawings by Caroline J. Potter)

Heap: Bobby adjusts his course and heads north to get around the cliff.

Complication #2: Trigger: Yikes! Big, BIG storm. Now what?

Heap: Bobby adjusts his course again and heads southeast, fleeing the storm. Pounding waves assault him.

Complication #3: Trigger: The storm broke his compass. Bobby's lost and very lonely. Treasure hunting isn't as much fun as he thought it would be, especially when you're alone. Should he turn around and go home?

Heap: Brave Bobby Boat keeps right on going. Whenever he feels afraid or lonely, he whistles a happy tune.

Major crisis: Stop!!! Double-take. What did he just see? Bobby goes through a paradigm shift. He adjusts his course once again, sailing back to the mermaid's rock.

Major structural climax/Major emotional climax: Bobby throws his map away. Who cares about gold? Real treasure is finding a friend. **Ending stasis**: they lived happily ever after, with the usual wavy ups and downs on life's uncharted sea. The end.

protagonist's choice ultimately leads to the **major structural climax** (heap). The major crisis occurs *at least halfway through the script and may occur just prior to the major structural climax.*

Where in the script does the major crisis take place? As a practical matter, the major crisis grabs audience interest, so it shouldn't happen too soon. It doesn't always occur just before the major structural climax, however. The script may contain additional complications between the major crisis and the major structural climax.

We noted earlier that a crisis is a point at which the protagonist has to think about choices. The major crisis is generally the point in the story at which the protagonist is confronted with his/her most important choice.

Another way to identify the major crisis is to look for a moment of significant discovery. Does this discovery cause important change for the protagonist? One of the most powerful types of discovery changes a character's belief about how the world works. Such a change in worldview is called a **paradigm shift.** If the protagonist undergoes a paradigm shift, that choice point will be the major crisis. The change of worldview itself causes the protagonist to make a highly meaningful, often extreme, choice.

Not all protagonists undergo a worldview transformation, but since many scripts embody a pattern of learning and change, we suggest looking for a paradigm shift. Ask yourself: What is the protagonist's worldview at the beginning of the play? At the end? Has the worldview changed? If so, what triggered the change? If you find the trigger for the paradigm shift, you have found the major crisis.

Major Structural Climax

The *single moment* when the protagonist does something that resolves the main action. You need to have identified the main action in order to recognize the major structural climax. Occasionally, someone other than the protagonist performs the final action. If the major structural climax doesn't follow the traditional pattern, however, you should ask yourself why the playwright chose this particular deviation. An unusual structural climax calls audience attention to itself and influences the meaning of the play. See the analysis of *Tartuffe* in Chapter 7 for an example.

Major Emotional Climax

The *single moment* that is the emotional highpoint of the story for the audience. If you choose to play the **emotional climax** at the same moment as the structural climax, the intensity emphasizes the significance of the protagonist's final choice.

Whether they occur together or at different times, each type of climax must happen in a moment. An audience can only endure climactic intensity for a short time. Inexperienced actors have a tendency to hit the emotional peak too soon, thus a whole scene can turn into a yelling match, while the audience turns off and tunes out. The later in the script the major structural and emotional climaxes occur, the more effective you are as an artist: End with a bang, not a fizzle.

Ending Stasis

A new state of balance at the end of a script: the situation created by the major structural climax.

How do I decide if it's the major crisis or the major climax?

Some script analysis systems do not use the term "major crisis." In that case, the analyst may identify what we would call the major crisis as, instead, the major climax.

When the shepherd (who is also the witness to Laius's death) appears on the scene, Oedipus forces him to confess the awful truth: that Oedipus is not only the killer of Laius but Laius's son. The moment when Oedipus learns he has killed his father and married his mother, thus fulfilling the destiny he tried to escape, is a huge emotional peak. If you've studied *Oedipus* before, your teacher may have said Oedipus's discovery of the truth is the climax. If your teacher applied Freytag's pyramid, this analysis fits. Freytag puts the climax in the middle of the script.

But there's a lot of script left after that revelation. If Oedipus's discovery is the climax, the rest of the play will be anti-climactic, therefore boring. Why would a playwright make this mistake? What director or actor would want to play the climax too early and then bore the audience? For a practicing theatre artist, Freytag's model with the climax in the middle doesn't work.

Could Oedipus's discovery of who he is be considered the *major crisis* of the script? Does Oedipus go through *a paradigm shift* because of his discovery?

- Before the moment of truth, Oedipus believed his adopted parents were his real parents. He finds out he didn't know who he was.
- Before his discovery, Oedipus was an honored king. He learns that he is the criminal who caused the plague in Thebes: he has committed patricide and incest. His social and moral status goes from the highest to the lowest.
- Oedipus hadn't believed in fate — or at least, he thought fate could be escaped. Now he discovers that in the very act of trying to escape his fate, he has fulfilled it.

Oedipus's whole idea of the way the universe works has been turned inside out. Oedipus's paradigm shift is about as extreme as a paradigm shift can get.

Changing one's worldview, as we see in the play, can be painful. If you haven't yet undergone this transformation, you may be glad when you do that Sophocles wrote *Oedipus the King*. Oedipus's paradigm shift can also be used as an analogy for the transition from one stage of critical thinking to another. Remember: the first stage is "Colonel Quaritch," in which one believes in absolute truths. A world of absolute truths feels secure. Leaving each developmental stage and ascending to another level of critical thinking poses challenges to us similar to the challenge Oedipus faces.

Furthermore, Oedipus's action hasn't yet ended once he has discovered the truth about himself. He must choose: What will he do, now that he realizes who he is and what he has done? Sophocles must have thought what Oedipus does after he learns the truth is meaningful, or he would have ended with Oedipus's discovery. If Oedipus's discovery that he has fulfilled his destiny triggers the major crisis, then his choice to blind himself and place himself in the hands of the gods could be viewed as the heap. Oedipus blinds himself offstage, however, and other scenes follow the blinding. The script challenges theatre artists to make choices themselves as they seek to identify the major climaxes.

If you read different scholars, you will find that some call Oedipus's discovery the climax, while others call it the crisis. One critic is not "right" and the other "wrong." The critics have different understandings of how a script is structured.

We encourage you to use the concepts of "major crisis," "structural climax," and "emotional climax," even if you previously learned Freytag's model with the climax in the middle. The "major crisis" version of dramatic structure is *useful* for theatre artists who want to create an exciting production that won't let the audience doze off halfway through the show.

1. Think about your favorite plays and films. Can you think of one in which the main character goes through a paradigm shift?
2. Write a concise analysis of the major crisis of that story.
3. What event triggers the crisis?
4. What discovery does the character make?
5. How does that discovery change the character?
6. What choice does the character make in response to the discovery?

or

1. Have you ever undergone a paradigm shift in your own life?
2. If so, write a brief analysis of that crisis in your own life story.
3. Answer the questions above as if you were a character in a script.

EXERCISE 3:4
Paradigm shift

In chapter one of this text, we mentioned the value of "thinking through" a process with an expert in a field of study. Below is an example of structural analysis by an experienced script analyst. We have chosen *Avatar* for analysis, even though *Avatar* is a film rather than a play. Films and plays differ in the medium through which they tell a story but both use a script that needs interpreting. Some film scripts, like some theatre scripts, use alternative structures, but *Avatar* follows the traditional narrative structure we explore in this text. The author directed the film, so the production presumably reflects the screenplay. We suggest viewing the film before reading the analysis, preferably the first version that appeared in the cinema, since the analysis is based on that version.

Example 3:1: Thinking Through Key Structural Elements of *Avatar*

An expert at script analysis doesn't read a script and magically come up with an interpretation. Like the beginner, the experienced analyst reads the script a number of times and asks herself questions. She writes down preliminary ideas and then revises them. The answer to one question affects the answer to another. Below, we follow the thinking process of an experienced analyst approaching *Avatar*:

- **Analysis: Choice of protagonist:** The film tells the story of Jake Sully. His character also changes the most. There are no other options for protagonist, so this decision is easy.
- **Analysis: Major Crisis:** Usually, a beginner starts by identifying the main action. After seeing the film four times and the Blu-ray six times, I have an idea about what *Avatar* means. I'll talk about meaning in another chapter. However, having a thematic idea, I find myself drawn to the question: Where's the major crisis?
  a. During the film, Jake seems to shift from the corporate colonies' model of reality to the Na'vi worldview — a significant paradigm shift. Where does that shift happen?
  b. Change gradually occurs over a series of scenes: Jake learns about the forest, proves himself a man, and is accepted as "one of the people."
  c. However, even after mating with Nateyri, Jake still asks himself, "What are you doing?" The paradigm shift isn't complete.
  d. What if the major crisis were the destruction of Home Tree by the corporate colonizers? Does the full paradigm shift happen then for Jake?

- **Evaluation:** The destruction of Home Tree seems right for the major crisis. From that point on, Jake stops trying to follow the colonizers' orders. His full loyalty shifts to the Na'vi. The fall of Home Tree also is a highly intense scene in the film.
- **Creating Main action, 1st draft:** "Jake wears an avatar body in order to spy on the Na'vi for the Colonel and figure out a way to get them to leave Home Tree so the corporation can harvest the rich deposit of unobtainium, but he later switches sides and leads the Na'vi in defeating Jake's own race."
- **Evaluation:** This main action statement reflects a "story level"

analysis. In other words, it's a summary of events of the story. For now, I'll work with this main action and see where it leads me.

- **Analysis and Evaluation: Major Structural Climax:** Hmm. According to the main action I've written, the major climax should occur when Jake kills the Colonel. However, looking closely at the film, I see that Nateyri, not Jake, shoots the Colonel. I'm not satisfied with a choice in which the protagonist himself doesn't resolve the story's action. For now, I'll note this possibility, but I want to think more about the structural climax.

- **Analysis and Evaluation: Inciting incident:** I'm struggling with this choice.

    a. Does the inciting incident occur when the Colonel asks Jake to spy for him? Probably not; Jake has decided to wear the avatar before he meets the Colonel. So he really isn't wearing the avatar to help the Colonel, is he? I need to re-think how I state the main action.

    b. What about the first time Jake is told to put on the avatar? … Probably not: Jake has decided to wear the avatar before he came to Pandora, or he wouldn't be there. If wearing the avatar is essential to the main action, putting it on isn't the inciting incident.

    c. The inciting incident is probably the corporate agents' offering Jake the opportunity to take over his dead brother's job. I'm reluctant to make this choice because the scene is sort of a flashback to before the film began. Also, this sequence occurs extremely early in the film. Finally, we don't see Jake actually accept the position. He does say in voice-over, "One life ends and another begins." In spite of my reservations, the job offer seems the best choice for inciting incident — at least for now.

What are the criteria for structural analysis?

A. Stasis

   1. The beginning stasis is the *situation* as it exists before the script starts. It should not include any action that happens in the first scene.

2. The stasis includes all major given circumstances relevant to the situation, even if the reader doesn't get some of that information until later in the story.

3. The stasis includes back-story relevant to the main action the protagonist takes.

B. Inciting Incident

1. The inciting incident is the specific *event* that triggers the main action of the story, and usually stimulates the protagonist into action.

2. Exposition mustn't be confused with the inciting incident. The inciting incident normally doesn't come at the very beginning of the script because the playwright needs time to describe the stasis. If the inciting incident you've identified doesn't trigger the main action, it isn't the inciting incident.

3. The inciting incident must be an event that occurs within the script itself, not something that happens before the script starts.

4. The inciting incident must include both *the trigger* and *the heap*. Make it clear *how* the inciting incident triggers the main action (heap).

C. Major Complications

1. The *main action* is the action you should trace through the series of complications, major crisis, and major climaxes. You should show how each structural element relates to that main action.

2. Each complication should be *numbered*.

3. You should include both the *trigger and heap* for each complication. Both trigger and heap must be *actions*, not feelings. Clearly show how the trigger causes the heap.

4. A trigger is almost always something an antagonist or ally does. A heap is almost always something the protagonist does in response to the trigger. Exceptions may occur when a major complication occurs outside the protagonist's presence, if the consequence then serves as a trigger to change the protagonist's course of action.

5. A script can have numerous major complications.

6. Major complications can sometimes happen after the *major crisis.*

D. Major Crisis

1. The major crisis must include the *major complication* that triggers it and the choices facing the protagonist.
2. You need to *justify* your choice in terms of how the major crisis leads (ultimately or immediately) to the *major structural climax.*
3. If the major crisis is a *paradigm shift* or other major discovery for the protagonist, you should say so and explain why.
4. If the protagonist undergoes a paradigm shift, that discovery and the choices it engenders will be the *major crisis* of the play.
5. Does the major crisis occur at least halfway through the play? If not, it's not the major crisis.

E. Major Structural Climax

1. Justify your choice of *major structural climax* by showing how it resolves the main action of the play.
2. The major structural climax must occur in *a single moment.* Make it clear which specific moment you're identifying. If you say, "the moment she decides to. . ." you must point out where in the script that decision occurs.
3. The major structural climax must occur close to the end of the script.

F. Major Emotional Climax

1. Your choice of major emotional climax should be justified with an explanation of how this moment provides the emotional peak of the story for the audience.
2. The major emotional climax must occur in *a single moment.* Make it clear *which* single moment.
3. The major emotional climax should occur close to the end of the script. It *may* occur at the same time as the structural climax. Even if it does, justify this event as the emotional climax.

G. End Stasis

The ending stasis should describe the *situation* at the end of
the script, after the action has ended.

Capstone Assignment: Structural Analysis

Try doing a structural analysis of a script in outline form. You might
choose the script, or your teacher might assign one. The script chosen should
follow traditional Western linear organization. For this first attempt, the script
should be reasonably straightforward in structure. Shakespearean plays with
lots of subplots aren't a good place to start. Below you will find a form to lead
you through a structural analysis outline. Add space as needed to insert as
many major complications as you find in the script you are analyzing. Finish
with your structural outline of the script.

Part A: Analysis

1. Read the script more than once.
2. Who is the protagonist?
3. What is the protagonist's goal?
4. What main action does the protagonist take in pursuing that
    goal?
5. Now read the script backwards. See if you can identify the
    three most significant points in the script's structure:
    a. the major structural climax,
    b. the major crisis,
    c. the inciting incident.
6. Which of the three is easiest for you to find?
7. Why?
8. Once you have decided on these three key building blocks, go
    back to see if you can find the major complications that lead
    from one point to another.
9. In this script, are there complications between the major
    crisis and the structural climax or not? Sometimes there are;
    sometimes there aren't.
10. Now think about the beginning and end stasis.
11. Which given circumstances are essential to what happens in
    the script: list those in your outline under "beginning stasis."
    Add significant back-story.
12. What are the most important things that have changed by the

end? List those under "end stasis."

13. Finally, consider where you as a theatre artist think the emotional climax should occur. As actor, director, or designer you can heighten an event's impact to make it emotionally climactic.

Structural Analysis Outline Form

1. **Stasis:** What are the key elements of the situation at the beginning of the play?

2. **Inciting Incident:** The significant event (trigger) that sets the main action of the play (heap) in motion.
   Trigger: identify the event that triggers the main action of the play.
   Heap: explain how the Inciting Incident triggers the main action of the play.
   What is the *Protagonist's First Step?*

3. **Major Complications:** Anything a character other than the protagonist does that affects the direction in which the main action moves. A major complication is often an **obstacle** but it may also be **unexpected help**. Complications may take the form of new information, opposition to a plan, or the actions of characters. A major complication is composed of a major trigger and heap. Identify the major complications by numbering them and identifying the trigger and heap for each one.

4. **Major Crisis:** The turning point when the protagonist must make a choice that leads to the ending of the story. It is the most significant complication (trigger) leading to the major structural climax (heap). The major crisis occurs *at least halfway through the script and may occur just prior to the major structural climax.*
   Trigger: What event triggers the crisis?
   Justification: What choices is the protagonist faced with? What choice does the protagonist make? Why (If there is a *paradigm shift*, explain it)? How does that choice ultimately lead to the major structural climax?

5. **Major Complication(s) After Major Crisis:** If there are major complications following the major crisis, analyze them using the format for major complications given above.

6. **Major Structural Climax:** The *single moment* when the pro-

tagonist does something that resolves the main action. In special cases, someone other than the protagonist takes the final action. *Identify* the single moment in which the main action identified in RAS is resolved.

Justify — how does this event resolve the main action?

7. **Major Emotional Climax:** The *single moment* that is the emotional high point of the story for the audience. If you choose to play the emotional climax at the same moment as the structural climax, the intensity emphasizes the significance of the protagonist's final choice.

   Identify the emotional high point of the story (single moment)

   Justify — why is this moment the emotional peak of the story?

8. **Ending Stasis:** Describe the new state of balance at the end of a script: the situation created by the **Major Structural Climax**.

Part B: Critical Thinking

1. Evaluate each element of your structural analysis according to the criteria listed for that element.

2. Start with the three most important building blocks: The inciting incident, major crisis, and major structural climax. Does each of your choices meet the standards? If not, look for better choices.

3. After reviewing and possibly revising your key structural elements, engage in the same process with the other elements: the beginning stasis, each major complication, the emotional climax, and the end stasis.

4. Comparing your work to the criteria for structural analysis is an essential part of the process of *critical thinking*. You have just used critical thinking in analyzing a script.

Part C: Mental Management: Reflection

Reflect on the structural analysis you've written. Answer the following questions:

1. How would you describe the thinking process you used to analyze the structure of your sample script? Identify as best you can the mental steps you took as you looked for the important structural elements.

2. How would you describe the thinking process you used to evaluate whether your choices matched the criteria? Choose

at least one of the criteria listed above and explain how you thought through your use of that criterion.

3. What questions do you have about doing a structural analysis of the kind you've just done? What don't you understand?

Peer Review Checklists for Capstone Assignments can be found in Appendix B.

Chapter 4:
Root Action Statements

What is a root action statement?

In the previous chapter, you completed a **story level** structural analysis. What we mean by "story level" is looking at the *individual* narrative in the script without seeing its *universal* implications. Now you're ready to learn a tool which helps theatre artists advance beyond story level. The **Root Action Statement** (**RAS**) is a single sentence which summarizes your view of the script's main action. Your own unique interpretation, thus your RAS, will differ from everyone else's. Validity of an RAS depends on capturing the essence of the script's action. Writing an RAS is thus one step towards thematic interpretation, our eventual goal as theatrical artists: What does this *story mean*?

How is an RAS structured?

The RAS has four interrelated parts:

- A description of the **protagonist** (noun and adjectives). The kind of person the protagonist is triggers the type of main action that occurs. Your analysis of the **given circumstance**s will help you describe the protagonist.
- A description of the **main action** the protagonist pursues throughout the entire play (action verb form). The type of main action triggers the major crisis and consequence/result.
- A description of the **discovery** or other **major crisis** the protagonist experiences. *If the protagonist undergoes a paradigm shift, that event is the major crisis.*

57

- A description of the **consequence/result** of the main action and major crisis. *The consequence/result corresponds with the structural climax of the script.*

All four parts must be related to and validated by evidence from the script. These relationships are expressed in a complete sentence composed in the following manner:

- "This script is about (**description of the protagonist**), who (**main action of the** script), but (**discovery/paradigm shift**) and therefore (**consequence/result**)."

EXERCISE 4:1

Creating a
story-level
root action
statement

1. If you did the Capstone Assignment in Chapter 3, you have already identified a protagonist, a story-level main action, the major crisis, and the major structural climax. Try putting them together for your first draft of an RAS.
2. If you haven't yet analyzed the four key structural elements in a script, please do that analysis for a script assigned by your instructor. Integrate those four elements into an RAS.

At the completion of this exercise, you have a story-level RAS.

What is "abstraction?"

In order to transform a story-level RAS into your unique interpretation of the script, you need to think abstractly. **Abstraction** is a thinking skill that makes thinking possible. Abstracting is so habitual we do it without noticing. Abstraction is the process of moving from the level of reality — the specific and concrete — to the level of concepts. My cat Deedee is a specific large fur ball with a loud meow. When I say "DeeDee," I'm talking about the only being in the universe that is currently sitting next to my laptop and purring.

However, the minute I stop using DeeDee's name and talk about "a cat," I've gone up a level in abstraction. There are millions of individual cats which are similar in some ways but different in others. If I say, "a pet," I've gone up another level. The classification "pet" is larger than "cat" and could include dogs, birds, fish, and hamsters. If I say, "an animal," I've gone to yet a higher level; the category "animals" can include wild critters as well as pets: foxes, cougars, elephants, and so on.

By abstracting, we lose specific details about DeeDee, but we are able to think about the things a particular class of beings have in common.

We use the process of abstraction all the time in our daily lives. Our minds put things into groups according to characteristics the groups share. If we didn't abstract, our lives would be unbearably chaotic. By putting things in categories, humans can begin to make meaning of our world and see patterns that enable us to predict what will happen in the future.

1. Think about something you're wearing today. Make a list of all the different ways you could abstract from it, according to its various characteristics. See how high up in level you can go.
2. Visualize the person you love the most. Make a list of all the different categories into which you could put this person.

EXERCISE 4:2
Abstracting in daily life

How do you apply abstraction to script analysis?

In the case of script analysis, abstracting seeks to move the script from an individual person's story (the story level) to a level of awareness that reveals a meaningful pattern of human existence (universal). The RAS is the tool we use to work through the process of abstracting the main action of the protagonist from the personal level to universal level. In the process of moving from story level to the more universal level of your RAS, each choice you make says something about how you're interpreting the script. What does the script mean to you? What truth about some aspect of human life is the playwright showing the audience in this script? You can see the process at work in the following example using *Oedipus the King*.

Example 4:1 Abstracting Up From Story Level

- **Draft 1: Story level:** "This script is about Oedipus, who searches for the killer of Laius, but when he solves the murder, he loses his kingdom and his self-esteem."
- **Draft 2: More abstract:** "This script is about a proud king who plays detective, but when he solves the crime, he changes his own life."
- **Draft 3: More abstract than story level but closer to an interpretation of the script than #2:** "This script is about a responsible ruler who searches for the cause of the curse upon

his city, but when he discovers he himself is the cause, he takes responsibility and punishes himself."

Be careful not to abstract so far that the statement could be an RAS for any script. "*Oedipus the King* is about a person who seeks the truth and finds it," for example, probably doesn't give an insightful interpretation of this particular script.

Figure 4:1

The Bull, by Pablo Picasso

2nd, 4th, 8th and 11th states. Read clockwise from upper left corner.

Picasso's famous "Bull" series, shown in Figure 4:1 demonstrates the process of abstraction in visual art. Notice that the first plate is not photographic realism; the artist is already interpreting what "bull" means to him. Think of the first image as the script, the second as a structural analysis, the third as a story-level root action statement, and the fourth as your refined RAS.

The Bull, **by Pablo Picasso:** 2nd, 4th, 8th, and 11th states. Photo: Réunion des Musées Nationaux/Art Resource, NY.

Let's take a closer look at how to think through the process of "abstraction." When you start to move up from story level, you have choices. With each choice you move closer to your own interpretation. For instance, let's imagine we have a script about a concrete, individual Macintosh apple. It is easy to move from the individual apple to the generic category, "apple," which includes all the individual apples in the world. However, let's say we want to "chunk up" a level and explore what "apple-ness" means. We have choices to make, as illustrated in Figure 4:2. We can interpret "apple-ness" in terms of its value as food, or *nutrition*. Now our story might encourage the audience to eat apples because they're healthy. A different interpretation of the apple story might be an exploration of how we experience apples through our senses. Now we

have "chunked up" in a different direction, focusing on how
we see, smell, touch, and taste
apples. A third possible path
for abstraction might consider
"apples" in terms of the particular symbolic role apples
play in this script. Each choice
helps you to move toward
an RAS that articulates your
point of view about the main
action in the script. A story
about nutrition means something different than a story
about temptation.

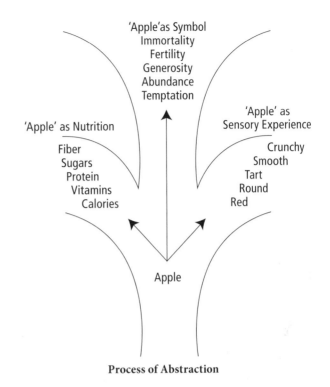

Figure 4:2

The process of Abstraction

Although the RAS itself is
not a statement of the script's
meaning, you want to make
choices that correspond with
your interpretation. In relating
the RAS to your interpretation, ask yourself the following
questions:

1. The script is about *what kind of person* (description of protagonist)?
2. What does this kind of person *do* (main action)?
3. What change does the main action lead towards (major crisis)?
4. What *happens* when this kind of person takes this kind of action and experiences this major crisis (consequence/result)?

How do you write an RAS?

You learn to write an RAS by writing one. Then another. Then another. Keep revising until your RAS satisfies you. Let's return to the RAS
in Example 4:1 and think through what each choice means in terms of
how we are interpreting the script. In these examples, we are working
with refining only the "description of the protagonist." In order to write
a complete RAS, you need to go through the same thinking process for
each of the four parts.

Example 4:2 Refining the Description of the Protagonist

- This script is about Oedipus, who ...
  Oedipus happens to be a king, but is "king-ness" the most meaningful description? If you choose the abstraction "king," that word brings with it associations of power and high status. Just by choosing "king," you interpret the script based on the protagonist's social position, power, or leadership: the script's meaning has something to do with rulership.

- This script is about a proud king, who ...
  By adding the adjective "proud," you indicate that pride is the protagonist's most important description, in addition to his being a ruler. The script's meaning arises from actions that proud rulers take.

- This script is about a responsible ruler, who...
  By choosing the adjective "responsible," you suggest the protagonist is the type of ruler who does his duty, probably taking care of the people he governs. The meaning of the script arises from actions responsible rulers take.

- This script is about a person who ...
  By choosing "person," you say the script's meaning applies to everyone. The actions the protagonist takes are things we all do, and the consequences can happen to us, too.

- This is a script about a proud person who ...
  In this version, you still suggest the protagonist could be any human, but you narrow the field to people who are proud. Since most of us, alas, have been proud occasionally, you imply the script might be a warning to all of us about the consequences of pride.

- This is a script about a son who ...
  By choosing the term "son" to describe the protagonist, you indicate that your interpretation of the script focuses on family issues.

And so on, through any number of protagonist descriptions. Remember, you need to go through the same thinking process for each of the four parts of the root action statement in order to unify the RAS.

1. Imagine that a script has been written about your life, from your birth until now.
2. How would you describe the protagonist — you?
3. What is the most meaningful noun that describes you?
4. What adjective(s) would you use?

EXERCISE 4:3
Describing
yourself as
protagonist

How do I unify an RAS?

An RAS must be **unified**. If an RAS isn't unified, it won't help you communicate a clear meaning. Being unified means all four parts must relate to each other in a causal manner. Who the protagonist is influences what she does, the main action. The main action leads to the result, as does the major crisis. Who the protagonist is also helps cause the result. Let's analyze one of the *Oedipus* RASes from Example 4:2 for unity.

Example 4:3 Analyzing an RAS for Unity

"This script is about a proud king who plays detective, but when he solves the crime, he changes his own life."

- *Description of protagonist:* "a proud king." As we've already observed, this description suggests that the script shows how pride affects rulership.
- *Description of protagonist + main action:* "a proud king who plays detective." Hmm. A king could play detective, but the way the main action is currently written, there's nothing linking rulership and pride to detective work. If we want to keep "a proud king," we should re-think how we state the main action.
- *Main action + result.* "Playing detective" changes the protagonist's life. Well … how does the action change the protagonist's life? In what ways? For better or for worse? Again, the relationship between the two parts isn't obvious.
- *Main action + Major Crisis/Paradigm Shift + result.* "Playing detective" could trigger solving the crime. But how does solving the crime change the king's life?
- *Description of protagonist + result.* "a proud king" whose solution of a crime "changes his own life." Hmm. How is the change (we're still not sure if it's good or bad) triggered by the protagonist's rulership or pride, but especially the two together?

This RAS doesn't seem *unified* — its four parts don't appear clearly related to one another, and none of the other parts seems triggered by the first — the kind of person the protagonist is. Let's see what interpretation the RAS we analyzed above might communicate:

- "This script is about a proud king who plays detective, but when he solves the crime, he changes his own life."
- *Possible meaning of the script:* "If you're a proud king, beware of solving crimes because it could cause major changes in your life. On the other hand, since we don't know if those changes would be good or bad, maybe you should jump at the chance to solve any old crime that comes along."

Does the statement of meaning given above accurately reflect your interpretation of *Oedipus the King*? If not, then the RAS we've been analyzing definitely won't work for you.

Let's look at an RAS for *Oedipus* developed by an experienced script analyst and check it for unity:

"This script is about a willful, spiritually blind man **(description of protagonist)** who seeks to wrest the truth from life with his intelligence **(main action)**, but when he discovers life is ruled by fate **(paradigm shift/major crisis)**, he surrenders to the will of the gods thereby trading physical sight for spiritual insight **(consequence/result)**."

- *Description of protagonist:* "A willful, spiritually blind man." The description of the protagonist suggests that the script will deal with spiritual or religious issues and how those issues affect all people (if we assume that "man" in this context is gender-neutral).
- *Description of protagonist + main action:* "A willful, spiritually blind man who seeks to wrest the truth from life with his intelligence." Hmm "wrest" means "to take by force," so the action seems compatible with the idea of someone who is "willful." The protagonist is relying on his intelligence to force life to reveal its meaning. Does a reliance on intelligence alone indicate spiritual blindness? Maybe, depending on the view of life demonstrated in the play. We need to look at other parts of the RAS before deciding whether the protagonist description

and main action are fully unified.

- *Main action + result.* The protagonist's attempt to use his intelligence to force life to disclose its secrets results in his surrendering to the will of the gods and giving up physical sight in order to gain spiritual insight. Hmm. Both the main action and the result have to do with the protagonist's search for the meaning of life, an understanding of how the universe works. The two together show a change: the protagonist thinks all he needs is intelligence to find the truth, but by the end he gives up that belief for an understanding that the universe is beyond his intellectual grasp and places his faith in "the gods" rather than human reason. These two pieces certainly seem related.
- *Main action + Major Crisis/Paradigm Shift + result.* Does the major crisis change the protagonist's view of the world and thus his behavior? Yes: the protagonist discovers that the universe is ruled by destiny, not human will. That change stimulates him to surrender to the gods instead of trying to control the outcome of his life by using his willpower and intelligence.
- *Description of protagonist + result.* The result of the script shows that the protagonist has transformed from an intellectually arrogant person who thought he could force life to conform to his will to a humbled being who now "sees" that life is spiritual and who surrenders his own goals to serve the gods' will. These two pieces of the RAS form a "before and after" picture of the protagonist's journey.

This RAS seems unified. Even though it was written by an experienced script analyst, it isn't perfect, of course. For one thing, it's rather long.

Does this RAS correspond with the meaning you find *in Oedipus the King*? If it doesn't, then even though the RAS is unified, it wouldn't work for you.

How does the RAS relate to the script's meaning?

As we've explained, the RAS describes the action that carries the script's meaning. Therefore, each of the four parts, and the unified RAS, need to identify your vision of what the playwright is showing about some aspect of human experience. As in your analysis of triggers and heaps, you may want to try working backwards if you think you have ideas about what the script might mean. Ask yourself: What issues does the script deal with? As an artist, which of those issues inspires me? Which idea grabs my emotions and demands I grapple with it?

If you think that *Oedipus the King* is mainly about *pride*, for instance, then your description of the protagonist might contain the idea of pride—such as, "This script is about a proud person who ..." On the other hand, if you think the meaning of *Oedipus the King* deals with *truth*, you might state the main action as, for example, "This script is about a _____ who searches for the truth ... "

EXERCISE 4:4

Thinking about meaning

1. Reflect on the meaning of the sample script for which you did a structural analysis, either in the Capstone Assignment for Chapter 3 or Exercise 4:1. Make a list of the subjects, issues, ideas, themes you think the playwright explores in the script.
2. Which of these topics seems most significant to you?
3. Why?

Let's look at another example of thinking through an RAS. This time, an experienced script analyst begins to develop an RAS for the protagonist of *Avatar,* Jake Sully. She begins with the main action she chose for her structural analysis, but she abstracts to make her RAS reflect her ideas about the film's meaning.

Example 4:4 Working on an RAS for *Avatar*

- **Looking Back at Main Action Developed for Structural Analysis:** "Jake wears an avatar body in order to spy on the Na'vi for the Colonel and figure out a way to get them to leave Home Tree so the earthmen can harvest the rich deposit of unobtainium, but he later switches sides and leads the Na'vi in defeating Jake's own race."

  I created this story-level main action statement in Chapter 2 so I could make a preliminary structural analysis. I knew at the time I composed it that it would need to be revised into a significant RAS.
- **Evaluation:** I have a place to start. Now I need to abstract my story-level statement in order to develop an RAS. I also notice that I didn't include a "major crisis" part, which an RAS has to have.

- **Analysis: Describing the Protagonist (RAS, part 1):** What do the given circumstances tell me about the protagonist? I know that he's a soldier, a marine, and that he lost the use of his legs in combat. So I might consider as a draft description of the protagonist, "a wounded soldier."
- **Analysis: Relating the Major Crisis to the Meaning:** The major crisis needs to go into the RAS, and often relates to a script's meaning. During my structural analysis, I identified that crisis as a paradigm shift, in which Jake changes from the earthmen's worldview to the Na'vi worldview. What is the difference between those worldviews? How does Jake's paradigm shift relate to the meaning of the film?
- **Analysis: Thematic Subject #1 and the Resulting Major Crisis (RAS, part 3):** A thematic idea that struck me the first time I saw *Avatar* is that the film draws an analogy between humans' pollution and destruction of our Earth environment and what the "sky people" want to do to Pandora: rape the land and murder people to satisfy corporate greed. So the film contains thematic ideas about "ecology" and "sustainability." Maybe what Jake discovers at the major crisis is that his own race are greedy murderers and the alien race take care of their planet.
- **Analysis: Thematic Subject #2 and the Resulting Main Action (RAS, part 2):** Another thematic subject, this one arising from given circumstances, is that Jake has lost the use of his legs. He is no longer whole. When he wears the avatar body, he can use that body's legs. He is more whole as an avatar than as a human. The Colonel promises Jake an operation to restore use of Jake's legs, if Jake can find a way to make the Na'vi leave Home Tree. Is Jake's main action a search for his lost wholeness?
- **Analysis: Thematic Subject #2 and the Resulting "Result" (RAS, part 4):** A third thematic idea seems central: transformation. Jake starts out by pretending to be a Na'vi; he's a human wearing a Na'vi body. At the end of the film, he permanently leaves his human body for the avatar body. He transforms from a human into a Na'vi.?
- **Evaluation:** I've come up with an idea for each of the 4 parts of the RAS. Keeping in mind my original story-level RAS, I try

out my ideas to see if I can "chunk up" (abstract) the RAS to a higher level of significance.

- **Creating *Avatar* RAS, 1st draft:** "The script is about a wounded soldier who seeks wholeness by pretending to transform into an alien native, but when he discovers that his own race are greedy murderers and the native race is ecologically sane, he transforms for real."

- **Evaluation:** Now that I have included a major crisis/paradigm shift, my RAS includes a *reason* for the "result." The main action leads to the paradigm shift, which triggers the final consequence. I've got all 4 parts, and the last 3 parts seem unified. Part 1, description of the protagonist, seems related to the main action but not entirely to the rest of the RAS. I need to see if I can do a better job of unifying the RAS.

- **Going Deeper:** I need to think more about the story. For one thing, "Wholeness" is an issue not confined to the physical. The Na'vi are energetically connected to the whole planet. They form part of a spiritual oneness that Jake lacks. I also want to tweak some of the wording.

- **Creating RAS for *Avatar*, 2nd draft:** "This script is about a crippled warrior who seeks wholeness by pretending to transform into a member of a 'primitive' culture, but when he discovers his own race is evil and the natives are part of a planetary spiritual whole, he transforms for real.

- **Evaluation:** The 2nd draft includes several thematic ideas. I haven't developed a complete thematic statement yet (see chapter seven) and I think the RAS will evolve further once I do. The RAS seems a bit long to me, as well. I think I'd like to condense it.

- **Changes in structural analysis:** After studying the relationship between my RAS and my original structural analysis, I would stay with my choices of inciting incident and major crisis. I would change my *major structural climax* to the last moment of the film, when Jake's Na'vi eyes open. This moment marks Jake's permanent transformation, having passed though death as a human body, and rebirth as a Na'vi.

One of the best ways to test the effectiveness of your RAS is to write out the meaning of the script the RAS suggests. Does that meaning coincide with your understanding of the script, the interpretation that would inspire your best artistic work?

1. Start with the story-level RAS you created in Exercise 4:1 above.
2. Abstract from story level towards the universal, as in Example 4:3 above, for all four elements of the RAS. Try writing a number of RAS statements until you get one you like.
3. Check to make sure your preferred RAS is unified, as we just did with the RAS for *Oedipus*. If it's not unified, revise it until it is.
4. Then write your interpretation of the script's meaning. Do the two match?
5. Is there an element in the RAS that doesn't have a corresponding element in the meaning statement, or vice versa?
6. If the RAS doesn't imply the script's meaning, keep working on both statements until you find a fit consistent with your interpretation.

EXERCISE 4:5
Comparing the RAS to your interpretation of the meaning of the script

What are the criteria for writing an effective RAS?

Although you have already worked with applying criteria in two earlier chapters, we recommend working through the following exercise before attempting this chapter's capstone assignment. The thinking required to create a valid RAS is more challenging and complex than what's required for given circumstances or structural analysis. In the preceding two chapters, you were mostly identifying, classifying, and analyzing. To compose an RAS you need to synthesize your previous analysis and create a statement that implies the script's essential meaning in action form.

Complete the following steps, in writing.

- **Criterion #1: The choice of protagonist matches the character whose story is being told in the script.**
  If the protagonist isn't easy to identify, the choice you make strongly influences your interpretation. Identify and justify your choice of protagonist. What criteria did you use in selecting your protagonist?
- **Criterion #2: The RAS has all four parts.**
  Write an RAS for your sample script. Highlight each of the

EXERCISE 4:6
Using criteria to evaluate and revise your sample RAS

four parts with a different color. Look carefully at your RAS.
Does each of the four sections of your RAS do what that section is supposed to do? If not, revise your RAS.

- **Criterion #3: The RAS is based on what actually happens in
  the script.**
  Reread the script. Does your RAS contradict any of the script's
  events or information? Are there essential events your RAS
  doesn't take into account? If the answer to either question is
  yes, revise the RAS to reflect the script more accurately.
- **Criterion #4: The main action is stated as a strong, active
  verb. You have identified the main action as what the protagonist does in this script, not something he did before the
  script started.**
  Look at the second part of your RAS. The action must be active
  — what the protagonist does, not what others do to him/her.
  If you're not sure what types of verbs are strong and active, see
  Chapter 5. Can you revise to make your verb stronger?
- **Criterion #5: You have abstracted the RAS beyond story level, but not so general that it could be an RAS for any script.**
  Is your RAS at a workable level of abstraction: beyond story
  level but still specific to this play? If not, revise it.
- **Criterion #6: All four parts relate so the RAS forms a unified
  statement.**
  Make sure your RAS is unified, using the steps given in the
  Oedipus RAS sample in Example 4:3. If your RAS isn't unified,
  revise it until it is.
- **Criterion #7: The RAS provides a step towards your interpretation of the meaning of the script.**
  Do your RAS and meaning statement match?
- **Criterion #8: The RAS correlates with the structural analysis.** The main action corresponds with the action triggered by
  the inciting incident, the third part of the RAS with the major
  crisis, the "result" part with the structural climax. If you have
  a "result" in the RAS along the lines of "discovers," "realizes,"
  "finds out," you're probably confusing the result with the major
  crisis.

- **Criterion # 9: The Root Action Statement should be clearly stated, easy to understand.**

  Ask a friend or a classmate to read your RAS and tell you what you've said — in his/her own words. Has your RAS clearly communicated your interpretation of the script's action?

Just look how much thinking writing a one-sentence root action statement requires!

If you feel you would like to see more examples, work more exercises, or read more information about root action statements and structural analysis, please go to Appendix A.

Capstone Assignment: RAS and Structural Analysis

Part A: Analysis

1. If you did the Capstone Assignment for Chapter 3, revise the structural analysis outline you wrote, adding the RAS at the beginning.
2. Trace the main action you identify in the RAS carefully through the outline.
3. Revise if the RAS changes your ideas about the structural analysis — or vice versa.
4. Now turn the outline into an essay. Justify and support your choices.
5. If you didn't do the capstone assignment for Chapter 3, do a structural analysis and RAS as assigned by your instructor.

Part B: Mental Management: Reflection

1. Did your RAS influence your structural choices? If so, how? Trace the thinking process as you made changes.
2. Conversely, did the structural analysis change something about your RAS? Explain what changes you made and why

Peer Review Checklists for Capstone Assignments can be found in Appendix B.

Chapter 5
Tools for Character Development

What kinds of thinking do actors use to create characters?

How do actors create characters? How can they generate inspiration when they need it? This chapter is designed to assist you in determining character development tools that work best for you. Before we can start learning the tools, we need to understand some basics of current acting theory.

Two basic approaches to character development are categorized as **inside out** or **outside in**. Constantine Stanislavski created the "inside out" approach, in which the actor analyzes the internal, or psychological, actions that fuel a character's external actions. The internal action drives the external action of the story.

The "outside in" method explores a character with kinesthetic thinking to get a feel for the character. Use of a voice, a walk, gestures, and costumes can stimulate this kind of thinking. Stanislavski, who continued to experiment with methods of characterization throughout his life, understood that "outside in" acting can be useful in the process of characterization.

Many actors use a combination of the two. Whether you're working "inside out" or "outside in," you need to understand psychological action. Actors who don't connect their character's external action to her psychological action often don't seem believable onstage.

In this chapter, we present an approach to character analysis drawn from Stanislavski's intense investigation of acting. Hating fakery and

clichés, he consciously developed tools designed to unlock the unconscious. His tools allow the actor to generate inspiration at will. To do so,
actors scour a script for clues to the characters' psychological actions.
These tools also exercise a variety of thinking skills from the analytical
to the creative.

What are character spines?

The primary tool we'll explore is what Stanislavski called a **character
spine**, a.k.a. superobjective. It is the main goal the character pursues
throughout the whole script. The spine provides a way of articulating
the most important psychological action driving the external actions of
the character.

What's the format for a spine?

We suggest that there are two essential parts to a character spine: the
strategy spine and the **goal spine**. The strategy spine describes *the way
the character goes about getting what he wants*. The goal spine identifies
what the character most wants to do.

Character spines are expressed using **infinitive verb** phrases. When
you choose a spine, ask yourself: Would I be excited to play this verb for
the whole two hours of the performance?

An example of the format for expressing a character spine looks like
this:

Character A wants to *strategy spine* in order to *goal spine*.

Your choice of verbs for your character spine is crucial. Verbs stimulate actor creativity. Also note that character spines use verbs in a very
specific way: in the *infinitive* form and the *transitive* form. Since verbs
are so important to creating spines, we should examine their use more
closely before applying this tool.

Why verbs?

Did you know that nouns and verbs activate different parts of the
brain? According to recent findings in neuroscience, verbs stimulate
the part of the brain that initiates movement, i.e., *action*. Verbs are action words. What actors do is *act*. Actors literally "enact" the verbs they
choose. Nouns and adjectives describe attitudes or dispositions and lead

to *showing* rather than *doing*. The point is not to *show* the audience what their character is doing but *to do it*. Working from the inside-out, actors use verbs to describe what the character is *doing* internally. This process stimulates an external behavior in pursuit of a goal. The behavior makes visible to the audience the character's internal action.

When actors describe the internal, or psychological, action of a character, they use an *infinitive* verb. Actors work with infinitive verbs because actors focus on the present. If my character's verb is "threaten," I can't use past or future tense, both of which would distance me from doing. Even present tense isn't strong enough. I look the other character in the eye and think, "I want to threaten you in order to force you to stop flirting with my husband, and I WANT TO DO IT NOW!" I loan the whole energy of my being to the character's will as I begin *to threaten*. The infinitive form of the verb is the most dynamic form.

Not all verbs are equally inspiring. Some are more dynamic than others. Some verbs just don't work for actors. Let's look at some types of verbs that do not serve the actor's purpose and compare them with some that do.

Which kinds of verbs are weak?

William Ball, in *Sense of Direction*, identifies several types of verbs to avoid.

- **Highfalutin' Verbs**. These words are too pretentious or intellectual. If you look in a Thesaurus, you're likely to end up with an unactable verb. Also, the word may not mean what you think it does. Examples*: to acquire, to bowdlerize, to abjure, to dandle, to disestablish, to discommode, to heft, to hinder, to homogenize, to humanize.*
- **Activity-But-Not-Goal Verbs**. Examples: *to recoil, to whimper, to giggle, to wait, to sit down, to eat, to fear, to sneeze.* These verbs just describe activity. Actable verbs, however, express what your character WANTS to do. Does your character WANT to whimper? To cower? To cry? Or might your character want *to hold back her tears* in order *to protect herself* from another character's mocking?
- **Passive, "To Be" Type Verbs**. Any verb that refers to a state of being is not actable. These words actually give the actor an

adjective to play, such as "to be clever." Find an active verb that conveys your idea. For example, "to be clever" might translate as "to manipulate"; "to become" might change into "to transform."

- **Instant Verbs:** This verb happens too fast for a character to pursue as an objective. Examples: *to slap, to kick, to hop, to twitch, to notice.*
- **Verb or Adjective?**: Actors may disagree about whether a particular verb in this category is actable. The issue: Verbs that seem too much like adjectives, leading to "showing" rather than "acting." Examples: *to charm, to pity, to grieve.* Imagine the stereotypical characterization if an actor plays "the grieving widow."
- **Wimpy Verbs:** *to talk, to tell, to question, to inform, to ask, to listen, to explain, to persuade, to convince.* These verbs are too general to stimulate an actor's imagination. Blah! They lack the specificity that inspires great acting.

What kinds of verbs are actable?

Actable verbs are clear, strong, appropriate, and as specific as possible to the situation. Some examples of **actable verbs** include: *to smash, to inspire, to seduce, to incite, to crush, to destroy, to ensnare, to tease, to reassure, to justify, to mock, to interrogate, to pry, to demand, to threaten, to blackmail, to evade, to flatter, to lay a guilt trip, to figure out, to humiliate, to punish, to manipulate.*

Seldom do actors discover just the right verb for the character's circumstances on the first try. Actors explore a series of verbs, making them stronger, more specific, and more actable with each draft. For example, here is a "wimpy" verb transformed into a more actable set of verbs.

Example: to ask — to request — to require — to demand — to lay down an ultimatum — to threaten — to blackmail — to dominate — to conquer.

In what circumstances might a character want to play each of these verbs in this escalating series of actions? The given circumstances of a scene, the kind of person the character is, and her relationship with other characters determine how forcefully she will act to accomplish a goal.

Try applying the "strengthening" process to your own work.

1. Choose one of the verbs from the "wimpy" verb list above.
2. Write out a series of verbs that transform it into a stronger, more actable verb.

Let's test our theory about actable verbs with this exercise.

1. You need a desk and two chairs.
2. Pair up with an acting partner. Designate one actor as the student and the other as the teacher. The rest of the group serves as audience.
3. The goal of the student is "to make the teacher give me a make-up test."
4. The goal of the teacher is "to refuse the student's request."
5. Given circumstances: Time: Friday, 4:45 P.M. Place: Campus office of the teacher.
6. Improvise the scene once using the infinitive verbs suggested in directions 3 and 4.
7. Each actor draws a stronger infinitive verb from a prepared pile supplied by your teacher. Do not share your new verb with your acting partner.
8. Play the scene again *doing* your new verb.
9. Each pair of actors shares the new scene with the audience.
10. At the conclusion of the new scene, the audience should try to guess what verb each actor was playing.
11. Questions for reflection/discussion: Which version of the scene was more interesting to watch? Why? Which version of the scene was easier to perform? Why?

How does an actor create character spines?

Everything we discussed in the section on verbs applies to character spines. Both parts of a character spine, the *strategy spine* and the *goal spine*, must be expressed with infinitive verb phrases that describe the *way the character goes about getting what he wants* (strategy spine) and *what the character most wants to do* (goal spine). Let's begin by working through an example. In earlier chapters we've thought about the character of Oedipus, so we'll start there.

The RAS we have previously written can be a useful starting place when creating a *character spine*. Our RAS for Oedipus is:

> "This script is about a willful, spiritually blind man who seeks to wrest the truth from life with his intelligence, but when he discovers life is ruled by fate, he surrenders to the will of the gods thereby trading physical sight for spiritual insight."

In this interpretation, Oedipus's main action is "to wrest the truth from life with his intelligence." A protagonist's RAS main action may be the same as either his *strategy spine* or his *goal spine*. Sometimes an RAS main action inspires spine ideas even if you ultimately choose other verbs to express your understanding of what your character wants and how he goes about getting it.

The RAS *main action* shows the protagonist relying on how smart he is to solve the murder, just as he earlier relied on his intelligence to escape his prophesied destiny. It seems that the main action corresponds with a strategy Oedipus uses, so that action might work as the *strategy spine*. To find Oedipus's goal, we must think about what he wants to do on a deep psychological level. Perhaps Oedipus's *goal spine* might be "in order to prove he's clever enough to outsmart fate." If we decide our analysis supports this interpretation, the entire character spine for Oedipus would be: I want *to wrest the truth from life with my intelligence* (strategy spine) in order *to prove I am clever enough to outsmart fate* (goal spine). This character spine satisfies the criteria we have so far identified as essential to a well-formed character spine:

- It is written as an infinitive verb phrase
- The verb choices are strong, actable, and gutsy
- It has a *strategy spine* (the way the character goes about getting what he wants)
- It has a *goal spine* (what the character wants to do)

EXERCISE 5:3
Using the RAS as a jumping-off point for developing character spines

1. Look again at the RAS you wrote as a response to the last chapter. Imagine you have been cast as the protagonist in that script.
2. What might your character's strategy spine be?
3. What might be his/her goal spine?
4. Justify your choices.

The RAS alone doesn't provide you with all the information you need to create a dynamic character spine. That's because the RAS is a tool that helps the artistic team discuss possible meanings of the *story*. It focuses on major events in the script's structure. Character spines are primarily *actors'* tools. Spine choices unify the character and guide the actor in choosing what s/he wants to do and how s/he wants to do it for every single moment the character is onstage. Creating spines demands going way beyond story level; it means probing deeply into character psychology. The character spine is a concise summary of deep analytical and creative work completed by the actor.

How do I harvest clues from the script?

Character development starts with script analysis. In this section of the chapter, we're going to work through a series of exercises designed to reveal a character's psychological action at a deep level. You may find some processes more useful than others. We suggest you try all the exercises in order to find the ones that work best for you. All of them should yield useful clues.

1. From the dramatic text your teacher chooses for this chapter's exercises, choose a character you would like to play.
2. Read the script focusing on the perspective of your chosen character.
3. Answer the following questions about your character.
   a. What given circumstances affect your character?
   b. How do these circumstances shape your character?
   c. What does the playwright say about your character in the stage directions?
   d. What do the other characters say about your character?
   e. What does your character say about himself?
   f. What does the character *do*?
4. Next, determine the accuracy, validity, and reliability of the information you've harvested. A thorough understanding of the given circumstances of a scene is essential to figuring out the meaning of the dialogue. Keep the following cautions in mind when deciding how much weight to give each source.
   a. The character may lie about himself.
   b. The character may not be very self-aware.

EXERCISE 5:4

Investigating the script

c. Other characters may reflect their own bias or misconceptions in judging your character.

d. Other characters may lie about your character to achieve their own goals.

e. Not all characters may be aware of all the given circumstances.

f. Ultimately, what a character *does* — his **actions** — provide the best sources of insight into that character.

5. Based on the clues you have harvested, how would you answer the following:

a. What do the clues suggest about the character's psychology?

b. What is the most significant *want* your character has?

c. Why does he want to do this action?

d. What does he *need*?

e. Why does he need to do this action?

f. What lack in the character's psyche do his actions fill?

EXERCISE 5:5

Creating an RAS as a jumping-off point

Write a root action statement for your character, as if she were the protagonist. After all, your character sees herself as the protagonist of her own drama! The main action of this RAS may serve as a jumping-off point for your spine.

EXERCISE 5:6

Inner monologue

One of the acting techniques Stanislavski developed is called **inner monologue**, or *subtext*. Stanislavski pointed out, in real life, people never say all they're thinking. Onstage, the actors he saw too often paid attention only to the techniques of line delivery. To Stanislavski, such a mistake led to shallow, phony performances. He urged his actors to figure out what the character is thinking but doesn't say out loud — and to think those thoughts while performing. In order to experience the power of inner monologue, try this exercise with your classmates.

1. To prepare for the exercise, write on slips of paper a sentence or two of "inner monologue" — what the character will be thinking while greeting the other character. Prepare enough for each actor in the class to use a different inner monologue. For example:

a. "I'll never forgive you for what you did to me!"

b. "I can't believe it! I just won the lottery!"

c. "What happened to you? You look awful!"

d. "Oh no! The last time I saw you, I made a fool of myself. What must you think of me?"

2. Pair up with an acting partner. Designate one actor as "A" and the other as "B."

3. The given circumstances of the scene: Place: a sidewalk.

4. Blocking for the scene: the characters enter from opposite sides of the space, meet in the middle, greet each other, and continue on their way.

5. Dialogue: Character A: "Hello, how are you?"
                 Character B: "I'm fine. How are you?"

6. Each actor draws a slip of paper with an inner monologue line before enacting the scene.

7. As each duo runs their scene, the rest of the class observes and then attempts to identify what each character was thinking.

8. Repeat till all actors have had an opportunity to run the scene.

9. Reflection/Discussion:
   a. Could you tell what the characters were thinking? How?
   b. As an actor, how did the inner monologue affect your performance?
   c. How might you apply this idea in your everyday life?

Finding a character's inner monologue helps an actor get beyond story level. It reveals why a character says each line. That insight can help the actor determine whether a character is sincere or sarcastic, lying or truthful.

Inner monologue can include mental images in addition to words. An actor must create specific images for every event he talks about in the script. Unless the actor sees those images in his mind's eye, the audience won't find the character believable.

Stanislavski suggests speaking the inner monologue aloud can be a powerful acting exercise. Although this technique works best after lines are memorized, you can start by reading a scene from your sample script with a partner.

EXERCISE 5:7
Applying inner monologue to your character

1. Choose a partner whose character has a scene with your character.

2. Read the scene through once out loud.

3. Then read it again. This time, speak aloud your character's

inner monologue before you say each speech — and also during any transition in the speech. It will take more than twice
as long to read through the scene with each actor speaking
both her inner monologue and the character's lines.

4. Reflection/Discussion:
   a. What did you learn about your character's psychology?
   b. Are there parts of the scene in which you don't yet know
      the character well enough yet to invent inner monologue?
   c. Consider coming back to this exercise after you have
      completed the rest of the exercises in this chapter and writ-
      ten your character spine. See if your inner monologue for
      this scene changes.

How do I use creative thinking to inspire ideas for character spines?

Finding a spine for your character is as much a matter of creative as
of analytical thinking. Use the clues you found in the text as a foundation, but then engage your imagination. Read the script again from the
point of view of your character to discover the world of the play through
your character's eyes.

EXERCISE 5:8
Brainstorming
to stimulate
creative
thinking

1. Use the activities below to stimulate your brainstorming.
   a. Character Doppelgangers: Do you know anyone in real life
      who is like your character? What insights into the actions
      of your character does the person you know stimulate.
   b. Character Metaphors: Sometimes you can capture the
      essence of a character with a **metaphor**. For instance, we
      describe things by their innate qualities such as "My char-
      acter is a feather" or "My character is a lion" or "My char-
      acter is a nail." In just the turn of a phrase the listener gains
      an understanding of the whole character in all its complex-
      ity. What metaphors would you choose for your character?
      What color, texture, smell, taste, shape, sound, shape, ani-
      mal/plant, dynamic image best captures the essence of your
      character? Why?
   c. Visual and Aural Stimuli. Look at photographs and paint-
      ings. What images suggest your character to you? Listen

to music, possibly from the period in which the script is set. What rhythms and sounds remind you of your character?

    d. Outside-in exploration. Move through space as your character. What's the character's weight? Shape? Rhythm? Speed? Center of movement? Do any verbs come to mind as you move in character?

    e. Imaginary Interactions between Characters: Greet each of the other characters. What does your character want to do to each character? What is your inner monologue as you greet each one? What is the one thing you want to do to all the characters?

2. After feeding your creative imagination with these activities, think again about your character's psychology. What *need* drives him throughout the script; in his life?

1. Write down as many spine ideas as you can think of. Don't try to judge their effectiveness at this point. Just write them down!

2. Now give yourself time for your creative mind to digest all the ideas you've fed it. A new and exciting spine discovery may come to you in the shower!

3. Hang on to this list of spines; we will use it as a reference for this chapter's Capstone Assignment.

EXERCISE 5:9
Trying on
some spines

How do I create a character biography?

Stanislavski encouraged, if he didn't invent, the acting technique of creating a **character biography**. Starting from the given circumstances, the actor creates a whole imaginary life for the character. The actor can thus "remember" important experiences that helped make the character who he is. This fleshing out of the character enhances the believability of the actor's performance. In order to be believable, an actor must also empathize with the character. The key to empathy, in life or onstage, is Stanislavski's "Magic If." Ask yourself, "If I were this character in these given circumstances, how would I feel? What would I do?"

Clues in you: personal analogies

Stanislavski argued that when constructing a character biography, an actor draws upon his/her own life experience. If you find empathizing with the character challenging, search for personal analogies. Actors must be willing to probe into their own psychology, as well as the character's, to find analogies they can use.

You do not need to replicate the exact given circumstances in which your character finds herself. For instance, few actors who play Oedipus have killed their father and married their mother. Instead, you are looking for a personal experience that elicited a comparable emotional response. Remember that an analogy has at least four terms: My experience is to me as the character's experience is to him. Maybe your analysis suggests that shame is Oedipus's key emotion when he discovers what he's done. What experiences of your own have produced feelings of shame? The stakes may not have been as high as Oedipus's, but if the shame felt intense to you, your experience may work as an analogy. If, like Oedipus, you discovered after the fact that you had unintentionally done something shameful, the analogy would be even closer. You never need to reveal this personal analogy to anyone, but finding it may help you empathize with your character.

EXERCISE 5:10
Creating personal analogies

1. What are the significant emotions your character experiences with which you need to empathize?
2. Make a list of qualities, needs, experiences, etc. for the character. Then make a second list, in which you compare and contrast yourself to the character. In what ways are the two of you similar? In what ways are you different?

A spine trigger? What's that?

The most essential part of the biography for you to create is the **spine trigger**. What significant events in this character's past have shaped who he is? In particular, what has caused the need which the character attempts to fulfill by pursuing his goal spine? This cause might be a particular occurrence, such as the character being beaten for breaking his father's watch. It might be a set of circumstances, such as growing up in poverty. We call this event or circumstance the spine trigger. It helps if the same trigger causes both the goal and strategy spines.

The four most important criteria for creating a spine trigger are: 1) the past event or circumstance must be appropriate to trigger the spines you've chosen; 2) the trigger must be plausible in terms of the script's given circumstances; 3) the spine trigger must help you empathize with the character; 4) the spine trigger must assist you in playing the spines.

Sometimes the spine trigger is written into the story. In most cases, however, you have to invent the spine trigger. It need not be an exact replica of an experience of your own; however, you may find that creating a spine trigger for which you have a personal analogy will make it easier for you to play your character spines.

Example 5:1 The Relationship Between Spines and Spine Triggers

The spines and spine trigger should lead to strong character choices. For example, perhaps an actor playing Oedipus has chosen the spines: *to prove that I'm sure-footed in order to defy the fate that wounded me.* Remember the name "Oedipus" means "swollen foot." Baby Oedipus's feet were damaged by being bound together when he was left on the mountain to die. His adoptive parents have not told him the truth about his origins. In creating his goal spine, Actor A has decided Oedipus believes he was born lame and resents the fate that disabled him. Even when the spine trigger is a circumstance such as a damaged foot, creating a specific moment in which the need is driven home to the character helps. For instance, Actor A imagines that Oedipus didn't see his lameness as shameful until, as a young boy, he tried to compete in an impromptu race to impress a visiting princess. Not only coming in last but tripping and falling in the dust humiliated Oedipus. He saw the look of horror and pity in the young girl's eyes. From this moment forth, Oedipus vowed to conquer all challenges, physical or mental, and never to admit imperfection. Most of us can relate to an experience in which we discover that we're imperfect — or different in some way.

The strategy spine "to prove that I'm sure-footed" gives Actor A a physical action to play. He decides that Oedipus's wounded foot has always caused him pain, but the king forces himself to walk without a limp in spite of the pain. Constant pain may aggravate Oedipus's short temper. Furthermore, Actor A has interesting choices to make as the script progresses. Does Oedipus's leg hurt more and more as he gets closer to the truth? Is there some point — after Oedipus learns the truth — in which he stops trying to hide his handicap and allows himself to limp?

The strategy spine, "to prove that I'm sure-footed," also gives Oedipus a psychological action to play. He must protect himself from revealing humiliating weakness — by solving every problem, quickly and efficiently. He must be "fast on the draw" in a debate; he must demolish anyone who opposes him, and he must never, ever admit he's wrong.

The goal spine, "to defy the fate that wounded me," gives Oedipus a need to challenge the gods, as well as men. A spine of that magnitude fuels Oedipus's rage against the prophet Tiresias … and anyone who stands in the way of his battle against heaven. Then imagine the catastrophe when Oedipus must confront his failure and bow to the power of destiny.

The spine trigger affords Actor A opportunities to interact with other characters. The look of horror and pity in that girl's eyes so many years ago slashed Oedipus's self-image into ribbons. To see a similar look in someone's eyes (instead of the admiration he needs as an addict needs a drug), triggers the dreadful memory. Think of moments when other characters gaze on Oedipus with horror and pity: Tiresias, Creon, Jocasta, and the Shepherd. Even Oedipus's choice of self-punishment, blinding himself, may grow out of Character A's choice of spine trigger. Oedipus says he blinded himself because even after death he could not bear to look in the eyes of those whose lives he had destroyed.

What are the criteria for creating spines?

Creative thinking doesn't end with generating stimulating ideas. After using creative thinking to generate spine ideas, we use critical thinking to evaluate them. We may then discard some ideas and pursue others further. As we refine our spine choices, we move back and forth between critical and creative thinking. We need to learn the criteria for good spines in order to evaluate our choices. But first, since we plan to use some examples from Molière's *Tartuffe*, we'll give a brief synopsis of the script.

A middle class Parisian citizen named Orgon sees poverty-stricken Tartuffe praying in church. Convinced Tartuffe is a saint, Orgon takes the sly devil into his home and demands his whole family pay homage to the holy man. Naturally, the family is appalled, except for Orgon's puritanical mother, Madame Pernelle. Cléante tries to make his brother-in-law see reason but only succeeds in aggravating Orgon so much the latter announces his plan to make Tartuffe a permanent member of the family — by marrying him to Marianne, Orgon's daughter. Marianne, devastated, wants to marry her beloved fiancé Valère. The saucy serving-maid Dorine comes up with a plot to foil the dreaded match. Sensing that Tartuffe actually lusts for Orgon's young wife Elmire, Dorine arranges for Elmire to converse alone with Tartuffe. Tartuffe indeed makes a pass at Elmire, but Orgon's eavesdropping son Damis wrecks everything by popping out of the closet. Damis denounces Tartuffe to his father, but the wily hypocrite manages to turn the situation to his advantage. Orgon disinherits Damis and signs everything he owns over to Tartuffe.

Elmire vows to prove to Orgon that Tartuffe is a lying lecher. She hides Orgon under a table and sends for Tartuffe. Wary because at their first meeting Elmire had rebuffed his advances, Tartuffe at first resists her attempt at seduction. However, when he finally starts to get physical, Orgon is too shocked by Tartuffe's betrayal to intervene. At last, dragged out from under the table by Elmire, Orgon tries to throw Tartuffe out of the house. Tartuffe, however, reminds Orgon that *he* now owns the house, and can throw Orgon out instead. Furthermore, Orgon has given to Tartuffe for safekeeping some papers written by Orgon's friend, a political enemy of the king. Tartuffe blackmails Orgon, threatening to give this damning evidence to the authorities, unless Orgon leaves without a fuss.

The family rallies around Orgon in an attempt to save him, but the police come to arrest Orgon, accompanied by the triumphant Tartuffe. The tables turn, however, and they arrest Tartuffe instead. The king's officer reveals that the beneficent sovereign, who sees and knows all, will set things right. Orgon's family gets to keep their house, Tartuffe goes to jail, and Marianne will marry Valère.

If you have read *Tartuffe,* you'll have a better understanding of the characters than you can gain from a synopsis; however, you should be able to follow the examples we give as we explain the criteria for character spines.

1. Each spine must be stated in the form of *an infinitive verb phrase.*
2. Each spine must be appropriate to the character and that character's behavior.

3. Each spine must be a gutsy, actable verb that drives the character through the script.

   For example, consider the character Cléante, Orgon's brother-in-law. Cléante seems to be the voice of reason, trying to get Orgon to see the damage he's doing to his family by kowtowing to Tartuffe. On a superficial level, we might think of Cléante's strategy spine as "to advise." If we start with "to advise" as a strategy, what's Cléante's goal spine? He advises in order to … what? Maybe: to help Orgon's family. Hmm. This starting point leads to us to view Cléante as one of those "nice" characters, lovely people in real life but boring onstage. A noble, all-knowing Cléante with the spine "to advise in order to help" would make both audience and actor yawn.

4. Each spine must go beyond story level and reflect deep probing into character psychology.

   The script analyst must be a psychic detective. We always need to ask ourselves: What's in it for the character? What deep psychological need does the character seek to fulfill by pursuing his goal spine?

   If you read Cléante's lines carefully, you will see that he expresses intense emotional reactions to people he considers hypocrites, as well as those who go to extremes. In Act I, Cléante argues with Orgon about the latter's senseless worship of Tartuffe. Cléante's lines are short until, finally pushed beyond endurance, he bursts into a long tirade about false piety and the human tendency to go to extremes:

Cléante   I've heard that kind of talk from others like you.
            They want to make the whole world blind like them.
            It's irreligion just to have open eyes!
            If you're not taken in by fakery,
            They say you've no respect for sacred things.
            You cannot scare me with that sort of language.
            I know what I say, and heaven can see my heart.
            We aren't befooled by such performances;
            There's false devotion like false bravery.
            And, as you see upon the field of honor
            The really brave are not noisiest ones,
            The truly pious, whom we should imitate,

Are not the ones who show off their devotion.
Isn't there some distinction to be made
Between hypocrisy and piety?
It seems you want to treat them both alike,
Honor the mask as much as the true face,
Make artifice equal sincerity,
Confuse the outward semblance with the truth,
Esteem the phantom equally with the person,
Take counterfeit money on a par with gold.
Really, humanity is most peculiar!
Men won't remain in the balanced middle;
The boundaries of reason are too narrow.
They force their character beyond its limits,
And often spoil even most noble aims
By exaggeration, carrying things too far.
All this, Orgon, is only said in passing.

Just prior to his death, Stanislavski was in the process of directing a production of *Tartuffe*. He warned the actor playing Orgon that many performers had made the fatal mistake of playing the scene between the brothers-in-law as mere exposition. Oh no, said the master director, this scene must be played like a duel to the death in which, by the end, Orgon and Cléante want to kill each other.

Imagine how boring it would be to play the long speech quoted above in a tone of calm reason. And why would Cléante say all he says if he didn't feel passionate about it? Notice too that in the last line of the speech, Cléante realizes he has just gone much too far himself and attempts to cover up his lapse.

When seeking a spine for Cléante, then, you might consider playing him as a hyper-sensitive type, terrified by his own emotions, who has to force the world to conform to reason (*strategy spine*) in order to cling to his own unstable mental balance (*goal spine*).

5. Each spine must be one that you as an actor can relate to, a spine that will stimulate you to make creative, original character choices.

   As an example, think about how the spines we just considered for Cléante might inspire interesting acting choices. What specific words or actions might trigger Cléante's fears and threaten his balance? What might happen when that fear strikes: a fit of hiccups, perhaps? What psychological gestures might Cléante use to regain his endangered stability? Drinking a glass of water? Maybe a threat to his mental balance makes Cléante want to sneeze? Maybe it makes him itch all over, so he has to try to restrain himself from scratching. Among other things, *Tartuffe* is a comedy, but comic character business only works if it is rooted in character psychology.

6. Strategy spines may be more easily actable than goal spines. Some actors like verbs that, while meeting all the other criteria, also lead to physical choices. Earlier, we discussed the acting advantages of "to prove myself sure-footed" as a strategy spine for Oedipus. Physically-oriented verbs usually work best as strategy spines, not goal spines.

7. Goal spines should go even farther than strategy spines into the character's deep psychological needs and desires. "To defy the fate that wounded me," the goal spine Actor A chose for Oedipus, is also actable but doesn't lead directly to physical choices. It does reflect the trauma at the core of Oedipus's character.

8. Each spine must be a verb you can play with *all* other characters, not just one.

   For instance, imagine you're playing Marianne in *Tartuffe*, a young woman who always does whatever her father tells her to do. A spine such as, "to please Dad" doesn't work because you couldn't play it with your uncle, your maid, your boyfriend, etc. Why is Marianne so obedient? Maybe her strategy spine is something like: "To avoid taking responsibility for my own decisions." And why doesn't she want to take responsibility? … In order to … what? Keep asking yourself "in order to … what?" as you dig into the character's psychology.

9. The spines must be capable of being caused by the spine trigger you have chosen.

   So if you choose for Cléante the spine "to force the world to conform to reason in order to cling to his own unstable mental balance," what might the character have experienced that could trigger such behavior? We can see from what he says in the lines quoted above that two things which really upset

Cléante are hypocrisy (especially religious hypocrisy) and people going to extremes instead of behaving reasonably and moderately.

Perhaps we might develop a character bio for Cléante in which he attended a religious school. His schoolmaster, however, proved to be a tyrant who brutally punished anyone who disagreed with the master's extreme and bigoted views. A sensitive and intelligent boy, Cléante tried to protect other students from the sadistic bully's rages, but the beatings he took, combined with the hypocrite's pious justifications for the violence, took a toll on Cléante's mental health. Confrontation with an irrational and dangerous world led Cléante to attempt to keep his own feelings and thus his environment under control. Whatever spine trigger the actor chooses should help him empathize with the character and play the spines.

How do character spines work with the other tools of script analysis?

We see now that the RAS, the character spine, and the spine trigger are closely aligned and interdependent. Each stimulates and reinforces the other. The character spine is the central touchstone for the development of your character. It provides your character with a unity of goal and strategy that creates a plausible pattern of behaviors throughout the story. Let's work through an example that utilizes all three tools.

Example 5:2 Thinking Through Jake's Spine for *Avatar*

Starting with the RAS, an experienced analyst thinks through some possible spines for Jake Sully.

- **Starting with what I know:** This RAS is the 2nd draft: "This script is about a crippled warrior who seeks wholeness by pretending to transform into a member of a 'primitive' culture, but when he discovers his own race is evil and the natives are part of a planetary spiritual whole, he transforms for real."
- **Analysis:** At this point in the analysis, I am not clearly distinguishing between the goal spine and the strategy spine. I am trying to cut a path through the underbrush so I can start to see what Jake is doing and why.

a. **To seek.** What does Jake *seek*? What does he need?

b. **To seek wholeness.** Jake has a need. He feels incomplete. He has lost some essential part of his being. His paralyzed legs are an external symbol of a deeper psychological loss at the core of his identity. What might be that part of his identity that is missing? Legs enable a person to move — naturally without the need for machines. They also connect a person to the ground, thus "grounding" him in the natural world.

c. **To seek the lost connection to the whole.** This spine might be easier to play than the previous one. I feel that Jake has lost a part of his being and feels incomplete without it. However, "to connect" would give him a concrete, even physical goal. He can seek to connect to people, things in the forest, and Pandora's deity. As a Na'vi, Jake has a physical appendage that allows him to make bonds with people, animals, and the goddess, who is connected to the whole world. The wholeness Jake seeks may not just be a physical part of himself but a spiritual connection to the cosmic whole.

d. **To prove my worthiness.** Jake continually needs to prove himself: to Grace, to the Colonel, to the Na'vi. Everybody calls him "moron. If Jake feels he is incomplete and thus unworthy, proving himself could be an important goal, a way of transforming from a "moron" to a hero.

- **Creating RAS 3rd draft:** Based on the psychological probing I just worked through, I create the 3rd draft of the RAS: "This script is about a crippled warrior who seeks wholeness by pretending to transform into a member of a 'primitive' culture, but when he discovers his own race is evil and the natives are part of a planetary spiritual whole, he proves his worthiness and transforms for real."

- **Evaluation of RAS 3rd Draft:** My revised RAS brings me back to the thematic idea that this film is essentially a story about transformation.

- **Analysis:** I start now to look for dynamic and actable verbs that precisely describe what Jake wants to do. I consider the following: *to change, to transform, to metamorphose.*

    a. All three of these verbs mean basically the same thing. *To change* doesn't seem strong enough; one can change in small ways. *To metamorphose* is one of those highfalutin' words — unactable. *To transform* refers to significant change and has a magical connotation.

    b. In terms of criteria, "to transform" seems to me the most actable of the three. It also stimulates me as an actor.

    c. Now I am ready to start drafting parts of the character spine.

- **Creating the Goal Spine 1st draft:** "to transform into a being worthy of wholeness."
- **Evaluating the Goal Spine 1st draft:** This draft captures something essential about Jake's *need.*

    a. This goal spine captures the ideas of transformation, wholeness, and worthiness.

    b. It is consistent with the ideas expressed in the RAS

    c. Another draft will help me flesh out Jake's character in more detail.

- **Creating the Goal Spine 2nd draft:** "To transform myself from a lonely, crippled individual into a being worthy to connect to the lost spiritual whole."
- **Evaluating the Goal Spine 2nd draft:** I feel as if, with the latest draft, I'm getting closer to the spine I want to play and it is grounded in the given circumstances of the story.

    a. Jake's need is social and spiritual as well as personal.

    b. He feels somewhat alienated from his own people even before the film begins.

    c. His twin brother has died.

    d. He has lost a sense of oneness with community, leaving him lonely.

    e. He discovers the only way to heal himself, to transform, is to give himself in service to the social and spiritual whole.

    f. He risks everything to make that leap of faith, that flight.

    g. I think I've drafted a goal spine that could work for me. But what's the strategy spine? *How* does Jake go about transforming himself?

- **Creating Strategy Spine 1st draft:** "To connect (strategy spine) in order to transform myself from an alienated, crippled individual into a being worthy to connect to the lost spiritual whole (goal spine)"
- **Evaluating Strategy Spine 1st draft:** With this strategy spine, I can use the verb "to connect" as *a means* of transforming myself. "To connect" as strategy spine offers potential for interesting exploration and acting choices.
  - a. How do I connect?
  - b. Are there different ways to connect through different senses?
  - c. In what ways do different kinds of connections transform me?
- **Creating the Spine Trigger.** Remember, the spine trigger emerges as a part of the character biography and is consistent with my previous analysis and the given circumstances.
  - a. It would be easy to identify the spine trigger as Jake's loss of the use of his legs. Certainly, that event causes the physical "loss of wholeness." However, we are looking for a trigger that explains his deeper psychological wound that has caused him to "disconnect."
  - b. Might there have been an event earlier in his life that caused Jake to feel alienated and incomplete?
  - c. If I want to invent a spine trigger that will strengthen Jake's reaction to the destruction of Home Tree at the major crisis, what might that trigger be? What spine trigger might I create that allows me to use a personal analogy for Jake's sense of loss?

Based on the analysis in the preceding example, write a spine trigger for Jake Sully.

EXERCISE 5:11

Jake Sully's spine trigger

1. Review the last draft of Jake's character spine in the preceding exercise.
2. Search for any clue in the film that might lead you to a plausible spine trigger
3. Consider Jake's past experiences (not included in the film) in order to create a spine trigger.
4. Consider the following criteria for spine triggers as you think thorough your choices:

a. Trigger should be appropriate to the character spines
b. Trigger should be plausible in terms of the script's given circumstances
c. Trigger will help you empathize with the character
d. Trigger will assist you in playing the character spines.
5. How will the trigger stimulate your creativity as an actor?

If you would like to review more sample spine analyses before doing your own, see Appendix A.

Capstone Assignment: Character Spines

This assignment is an opportunity to demonstrate your understanding and application of tools introduced in this chapter. Use the character you selected from your assigned script. Imagine that you, the actor, are preparing to play the role.

Part A: Searching for the Spines

1. Return to the list of spines you created for your character in Exercise 5:7. Using what you have learned from this chapter, you are going to polish the spine of your choice.
2. From your list, choose the spine that you now believe best fits your character.
3. Look at the verbs in your strategy spine and goal spine. Do they meet the criteria for actable verbs?
4. Using the following criteria, see if you can polish your verb choices to probe more deeply into the psychology of your character.
   a. Each spine must be stated in the form of *an infinitive verb phrase.*
   b. Each spine must be appropriate to the character and that character's behavior.
   c. Each spine must be a gutsy, actable verb that drives the character through the script.
   d. Each spine must go beyond story level and reflect deep probing into character psychology.
   e. Each spine must be one that you as an actor can relate to, a spine that will stimulate you to make creative, original character choices.
   f. Strategy spines may be more easily actable than goal

spines. Some actors like verbs that, while meeting all the other criteria, also lead to physical choices, for example, "to throw his weight around." Physically-oriented verbs work best as strategy spines, not goal spines,

    g. Goal spines should go even farther than strategy spines into the character's deep psychological needs and desires.

    h. Each spine must be a verb you can play with *all* other characters, not just one.

    i. The spines must be capable of being caused by the spine trigger you have chosen.

5. With each new answer to the question, "in order to what?" ask yourself if you can go further. With each new, deeper goal spine, repeat the questions: What's in it for him? He wants to _____ **in order to** _____?

6. Make notes on your thinking process, including activities you used to generate spines, spines you considered, and reasons why you rejected or selected a spine.

Part B: Creating the Character Biography

1. Create a biography for your character based on the character spine you chose in Part A.

2. Building on the clues in the text, invent a life history for your character.

3. Decide on a spine trigger and other important events.

4. Based on your analysis, create the details of your character's relationships with the other characters.

5. Flesh out your character biography with other significant events in the character's life, including detailed visions of happenings referred to in the script. Small details can help make the character real to you. For example, which season of the year does your character prefer? Why? What activity does your character engage in when he/she is bored? Worried? Joyful? And so on.

6. Identify images that stimulate insights into your character.

7. Take notes on your ideas.

Part C: Oral Presentation of Character Biography

Your teacher may assign you to present your character biography orally, either in small groups or to the whole class. In this exercise, you "become" your character and tell others about your life; they will ask you questions, and you will respond in character. Choose the moment your character first appears in the script as the "present" moment. Try to play your character spines. If your character would lie, feel free to lie. Don't read from a paper; put down your notes and try your best to play the character. And don't break character no matter what!

Discussion/Reflection:

1. What did you learn from the exercise, both in presenting your own bio and listening to bios presented by classmates?
2. Did everyone working on the same character make the same biographical choices?
3. What happened when you were asked a question for which you hadn't previously decided on an answer?
4. Was there any time during the presentation during which you felt the character was speaking, not you?

Part D: Written Character Analysis

1. In your own voice as the actor, write a short essay in which you identify your chosen **spines**.
2. Justify your choice with a brief character analysis, drawing on clues in the script as support.
3. Identify and justify the **spine trigger** you've selected.
4. Finally, explain how the spines will help you play your character. How will each spine stimulate you to make interesting and significant acting choices?

Part E: Letter to Another Character

To which character in the script might your character write a letter? Why would your character write the letter? What does your character want from the other character?

1. Imagine that you are the character, and write the letter in your character's voice. Try to capture the essence of that character's speaking style, as shown in the script. Respect the given circumstances, including the historical period in which

the script is set.
2. Throughout the letter, play your character's spines; pursue the character's goal and use the character's strategy.
3. Include in the letter some imagined events from the biography you created, especially an event that does not occur in the script but which reveals something important about the character.

Part F: Mental Management: Reflection

Answer both questions:
1. Refer to the notes you took while doing your thinking process for Part A of the assignment. Which of the activities you used to generate spines were most fruitful? Why?
2. Review parts B through E in this series of assignments. Which did you find most helpful to you in empathizing with the character, which were most difficult, and why?

Peer Review Checklists for Capstone Assignments can be found in Appendix B.

Chapter 6
Scenic Units: a.k.a. Beats

What happens when we change focus from big to small?

So far, we've been talking about the whole script, analyzing its structure and the characters' spines. Now we're focusing in on smaller pieces of the script. The standard format for scripts divides the action into acts and scenes. Actors and directors chop the script into even smaller bits and put them "under the microscope." We call these bits **scenic units**.

Characters in scenic units continue to pursue the overall strategy of their character spines, but as we look into the microscope, we see their unit verbs focus on what they do and want moment-to-moment in the scene. We call these verbs **unit objectives**. Character spines and unit objectives share a similar structure: they both include verbs that tell us *the way the character goes about getting what he wants and what the character most wants to do*. The form for stating unit objectives mirrors the one for spines: to (**tactic objective**) in order to (**goal objective**). Here we call the *way the character goes about getting what he wants* a "tactic" rather than a "strategy" to reflect the interactive nature of moment-to-moment character relationships.

If we think of the character's spine as the backbone in a human skeleton, then unit objectives might be like finger bones. They're attached to bones attached to bones that are attached to the spine, but they also do the "hands on" work of going after the character's goal spine. You need to understand the character enough to have selected a spine before looking for unit objectives.

What is a scenic unit?

Within a scene, characters try different tactics to get what they want. A scenic unit is a small slice of a scene in which the characters' tactic and goal objectives remain the same. Each time a character switches tactics, other characters have to react, to adjust their own tactic objectives, causing a change in unit. For example:

Unit 1: A interrogates and B evades.
Unit 2: A accuses and B denies.
Unit 3: B threatens and A defends.

Goal objectives can change too, but the tactic objective is what other characters can perceive and so is most likely to change others' tactics.

Remember, scripts are based on conflict. Character A wants *to do something*. Character B wants to make Character A *do something else*. Character A and Character B have opposing goal objectives. Each uses tactics to achieve his goals. This clash of tactic objectives provides dramatic conflict.

Figure 6:1

Tug-of-War: unit objectives. Slick (left) vs. Buddy (right).

(drawings by Caroline J. Potter)

Slick: to suck up to Buddy (*Tactic objective*) in order to trick Buddy into letting down his guard (*Goal objective*).

Buddy: to buddy up to Slick (*Tactic objective*) in order to entice Slick into taking it easy on Buddy (*Goal objective*).

Slick: to spring the trap (*Tactic objective*) in order to humiliate Buddy (*Goal objective*).

Buddy: to hang on for dear life to his balance (*Tactic objective*) in order to defend his male pride against Slick's attack (*Goal objective*).

Slick: to demolish Buddy (*Tactic Objective*) in order to prove that he (Slick) is the Alpha male (*Goal objective*).

Buddy: to flatten Slick (*Tactic Objective*) in order to get revenge for Slick's dirty trick (*Goal objective*).

Scenic units are like tiny complications. They build a structure of rising tension within a scene leading to major complications which keep the tension mounting throughout the script. Structural analysis of the entire script gave us a **bird's eye view** of the rhythmic ebb and flow of tension in the story. Now, we're shifting our perceptual position to the **worm's eye view**.

Analyzing a scenic unit, then, requires you to synthesize information from the use of two kinds of tools we've been learning: structural analysis (complications) and character analysis (spines). Compared to major complications and spines, you're looking for teensy-tiny spines and teensy-tiny complications. But these small complications and spines bring the scene to life for the actors, thus for the audience.

Who uses scenic objectives and why are they important?

Analyzing scenic units helps both the actor and director. For the actor, studying units adds nuance and depth to the role. When the stakes get higher for the characters, a change in tactic objectives helps to heighten the intensity for the audience. Actors who play each unit's objectives usually appear more believable onstage than actors who don't. The actor who fails to do unit analysis may miss important character clues. She's likely to bore the audience, and herself, by playing a single objective throughout the scene. Ignorant of the scene's structure, she can't feel its rhythm. Actors who can't recognize unit structure often fall into "indicating" rather than "doing." Their acting lacks the specificity that communicates believably what a character wants.

Each character present onstage must have tactic and goal objectives, whether or not the actor speaks in that unit. An actor onstage with no objectives is a fish out of water. If actors don't have something *to do*, they can't act.

For the director, studying units orchestrates suspense, keeping the audience wondering what will happen next. Using a variety of tactics creates the flow and rhythm in a scene. In order to guide actors, the director also needs to understand what the characters do and want moment-to-moment. Directors and actors share the common language of verbs so they can communicate about unit objectives.

1. Return to Exercise 5:1: Strengthening Your Verb Choices.
2. Try the teacher/student improvised scene again with several pairs of actors and different infinitive verbs. Let the scene go on longer this time.
3. Discussion/Reflection:
   a. Actors, what happened when you had to sustain your verb over a longer period of time?
   b. Audience, what was your perception of the dynamics of the scene?
   c. Actors, did the verb you were playing change in the course of the scene? If so, why? If not, how did your performance feel to you?

EXERCISE 6:1
Strengthening your verb choices: take two

     d. Audience, can you identify any changes in the verbs that
       were played?

     e. If changes occurred, speculate about why the changes happened.

How do I identify a scenic unit?

In order to figure out units, draw on your structural analysis skills. Identify triggers and heaps. What tactic objective is each character playing? What causes one of the characters to change tactics? How does the other character respond? Draw a line on the script to mark the point at which you think one unit ends and the next begins.

Write down the tactic objective each character is pursuing in each unit. Like spines, tactic objectives must be stated in infinitive verb form. All the criteria for actable verbs apply to unit objectives. You need to probe into your character's psychology to identify her specific tactic.

In addition, tactic verbs are **transitive**. A transitive verb needs an object to act upon to complete its meaning. Thus the action is driven outward towards another character. These examples from *Oedipus* illustrate the first two ingredients in unit objectives. Your character is doing something (tactic objective) *to another character* (**target**).

- TIRESIAS: I want **to warn** (tactic objective) **Oedipus** (target)
- OEDIPUS: I want **to force** (tactic objective) **Tiresias** (target)
- JOCASTA: I want **to soothe** (tactic objective) **Oedipus** (target)

The next step is to ask yourself, "why is my character using this tactic? What is his goal?" Jocasta wants to soothe Oedipus *in order to …* *what?* Now let's complete the statement of objectives by adding your character's goal objective.

- TIRESIAS: I want to warn (tactic objective) Oedipus (target) *in order to prevent him from investigating the murder and thus destroying himself* (goal objective)
- OEDIPUS: I want to force (tactic objective) Tiresias (target) *to tell me the truth in order to show him who's boss* (goal objective)
- JOCASTA: I want to soothe (tactic objective) Oedipus (target) *in order to calm my own jittery nerves* (goal objective).

A fully identified objective has three parts: the character's tactic objective, the target of the tactic, and the character's goal objective. While your tactic objective is aimed directly at a target character, your goal objective may or may not be something you want that character to do. In cases of inner conflict, for instance, a character may want to do something to herself. Jocasta's goal objective in the examples above illustrates this idea.

At this point we have discussed tactic and goal objectives but the scenic unit is not complete without a **cause of change**. Remember, scenic units are tiny complications and, as such, they have a trigger and a heap. We want to make it as clear as possible how the trigger causes the heap, and how the two together change the tactical pattern. Let's look at an example of several scenic units.

Example 6:1 Tactics and Triggers and Heaps, Oh My!

Given Circumstances: Mother and child in a checkout line at the grocery store.

Scenic Unit #1

Child	"Mommy, can I have a candy bar?"
Mother	"No sweetie pie, it's too close to dinner."
Child	"Please, please, pretty please with sugar on top!"
Mother	"No, honey. You'll spoil your appetite."

Objectives:

Child: to beg Mother in order to stuff his mouth with sugar
Mother: to reason with child in order to justify her refusal

Cause of Change (**CC**)   *Trigger*: Mom gives a good reason not to buy the candy bar

Heap: Child, realizing from Mother's reasonable argument that begging won't work, tries another tactic that has worked in the past: to bribe

---

Scenic Unit #2

Child	"If you let me have the candy bar I'll eat my dinner."
Mother	"No."
Child	"And I'll clean my room and I won't ask for anything else for a whole week!"
Mother	"I said no and I mean no, young man."

Objectives:

Child: to bribe Mommy in order to trick her into giving him what he wants. He has no intention of keeping his promises.
Mother: to put her foot down in order to command that the child stop trying to manipulate her.

Cause of Change (CC)	*Trigger:* Mom has caught on to the bribery tactic; she has discovered that the child won't keep his part of the bargain. Annoyed that he would try this tactic on her again, she refuses.
	Heap: From Mom's firm tone, Child realizes that bribing won't work this time. Mom's refusal makes him angry. He ups the stakes and changes his tactic to threatening.

Scenic Unit #3

Child	"If you don't let me have that candy bar right now, you'll be sorry.
Mother	"Now you straighten up or you'll be grounded for a whole week!"
Child	"I'm going to scream and cry! I'll throw a big fit right here in public!"
Mother	"A whole *month!*"

Objectives:

Child: to threaten Mommy in order to control her.
Mother: to threaten Child in order to prove who's in charge.

Cause of Change (CC)	*Trigger:* Mom refuses to give in to the child's ultimatum. She asserts her authority and threatens the child in return.
	Heap: Child is astonished and hurt that Mom would threaten him. He changes his tactic to accusing her of being a bad parent (he's still hoping to manipulate her into getting him the candy bar).

Scenic Unit #4

Child	You're being mean!"
Mother	"Right. Your life is so hard."
Child	"You don't love me anymore!"
Mother	"Oh, poor little sad, unloved orphan child.

Objectives

Child: to accuse Mommy of being a bad Mommy in order to shame her into giving in.

Mother: to mock Child in order to dismiss his accusations as ridiculous.

The battle between Mother and Child may go on for another ten minutes, but you get the idea. Most units, however, are longer than the units in this example.

1. Read the sample scene above with a partner while arm-wrestling. Allow the advantage to move back and forth between you depending on which character is "pushing" harder to achieve her goal objective at that moment in the scene.
2. Try to match the way you arm-wrestle to your character's tactic objective, including making your strength correspond to how much your character wants to win.
3. Discussion/reflection: Did you learn anything about the scene and/or your character? If so, what?

EXERCISE 6:2
Explore scenic units by arm wrestling

How do I determine the length of a scenic unit?

Units can vary considerably in length. A script the size of a small paperback often has four or five units per page. A single long speech by one character should be divided into units. On the other hand, a unit sometimes lasts half a page. If you find yourself making each line or two into a separate unit, you're making units too small. If you go for a full page without a change in unit, you're making units too big.

Characters alone onstage engage in one or more units. Don't assume that if just one person is there, the unit doesn't change. A character may have inner conflict; different "parts of himself" may wrestle with one another. Let the following ideas guide your thinking about length.

- A scenic unit should have an identifiable beginning, middle, and end.

- The length is determined by the character's use of a given tactic.
- Signs that a scenic unit has ended include:
  a. The character has achieved her goal objective.
  b. The character has not achieved his goal objective so changes tactics.
  c. The character stops pursuing his original goal objective and begins pursuing a new goal.
  d. New information, circumstances, or characters are introduced into the scene which affect either a character's goal or tactic objective.
  e. One character has been driving the action. Another character "takes the lead." The power shifts from one to the other.
  f. A change in time or location.
  g. The scene ends.

You may find you have an intuitive or rhythmic sense of where units change (particularly after you've studied the script, characters, and scene). Try drawing lines with a pencil where your first impulse tells you each unit ends. Then go back and do the analysis. As you analyze, you may revise some choices. But it won't hurt to test your intuition!

How do I record scenic units in my script?

Study the sample unit analysis below from *Arms and the Man*. Note that the analysis is written on a separate page facing a page of text. A line divides the units on the script page. A number matches the script unit to its analysis. This format, the one directors use, makes the analysis easy to read providing for efficient use during rehearsals.

The scenic unit analysis has two main parts.

1. **Character Objectives.** Identify the tactic objective, target, and goal objective each character pursues in this unit. Use infinitive verb phrases. The tactic objective comes first, then the target, then the goal objective follows the phrase "in order to." You may add notes to expand upon your insights into character psychology.

2. **Cause of Change (CC):** Here, you identify the trigger and heap that alter the motivational dynamics in the scene. Al-

most always, the CC occurs at the end of the unit rather than being spread out through the whole unit. *The CC at the end of unit 1 leads into unit 2, and so on.*

Note: In some units the trigger is specific and even obvious. In other units, you have to think harder. In still other units, you may need to invent movement or business to trigger the change.

Example 6:3 Scenic Unit Analysis

Arms and the Man analysis

32

> *Bluntschli* — to pacify Raina in order to control her. He genuinely appreciates her help. He also needs her continued assistance. Now that the immediate danger has been averted, the two combatants are sizing each other up and maneuvering for power.
>
> *Raina* — to put Bluntschli in his place and hold him at arms' length — in order to control him. He mustn't presume that just because she's saved him, she's now in his power.
>
> ### *Cause of Change (CC):*
>
> *Trigger:* Raina's claim that she's generous allows Bluntschli to take her measure.
>
> *Heap:* He decides to play the diplomatic guest in order to put her in the hostess role, a role in which she's duty-bound to offer him a safe haven.

Act I *Arms and the Man*

The Officer	Could anyone have got in without your knowledge? Were you asleep?
Raina	No: I have not been to bed.
The Officer	(*impatiently, coming back in to the room*) Your neighbors have their heads so full of runaway Serbs that they see them everywhere. (*Politely*) Gracious lady: a thousand pardons. Goodnight. (*Military bow, which Raina returns coldly. Another to Catherine, who follows him out.*)
Raina	(*Closes the shutters. She turns and sees Louka, who has been watching the scene curiously.*) Don't leave my mother, Louka, until the soldiers go away. (*Louka glances at Raina at the ottoman, at the curtain; then purses her lips secretively, laughs insolently, and goes out. Raina, highly offended by this demonstration, <u>follows her to the door, and shuts it behind her with a slam, locking it violently.</u>*
	The Man immediately steps out from behind the curtain, sheathing his sabre, and closes shutters. Then, dismissing the danger from his mind in a businesslike way, he comes affably to Raina.)
The Man	A narrow shave; but a miss is as good as a mile. Dear young lady; your servant to the death. I wish for your sake I had joined the Bulgarian army instead of the other one. I am not a native Serb.
Raina	(*Haughtily*) No: you are not one of the Austrians who set the Serbs on to rob us of our national liberty, and who officers their army for them. We hate them!

32

33

Bluntschli — to request Raina's hospitality, in as genteel a manner as possible, in order to charm Raina into protecting him. Masks go on as both guest and hostess dance a politeness waltz.

Raina — to play hostess to Bluntschli, graciously granting the guest's request, in order to impress Bluntschli with her manners.

CC:

Trigger: Raina sits on the pistol and gives a frightened shriek.

Heap: Bluntschli, unnerved, runs for cover.

34

Bluntschli — to chastise Raina for scaring him, in order to calm his panic.

Raina — to justify herself to Bluntschli in order to calm her panic. Frightened and irritated, each casts blame for their display of fear on the other.

CC:

Trigger: Raina judges Bluntschli as an oaf too dumb to understand a genteel woman's sensitivities.

Heap: Raina starts feeling superior to Bluntschli, and thus safer.

The Man	Austrian! Not I. Don't hate me, dear young lady. I am a Swiss, fighting merely as a professional soldier. I joined the Serbs because they came first on the road from Switzerland. Be generous: you've beaten us hollow.
Raina	Have I not been generous?
The Man	Noble! Heroic! But I'm not saved yet. This particular rush will soon pass through; but the pursuit will go on all night by fits and starts. <u>I must take my chance to get off in a quiet interval.</u>

33

	(*Pleasantly*) You don't mind my waiting just a minute or two, do you?
Raina	(*Putting on her most genteel society manner*) Oh, not at all. Won't you sit down?
The Man	Thanks (*He sits on the foot of the bed. Raina walks with studied elegance to the ottoman and sits down. <u>Unfortunately she sits on the pistol, and jumps up with a shriek. The</u>*

34

	Man, all nerves, shies like a frightened horse to the other side of the room. Irritably) Don't frighten me like that. What is it?
Raina	Your revolver! It was staring that officer in the face all the time. What an escape!
The Man	(*Vexed at being unnecessarily terrified.*) Oh, is that all?
Raina	(*Staring at him rather superciliously as she conceives a poorer and poorer opinion of <u>him and feels proportionately more and more at her ease.</u>*)

35

Raina — to challenge Bluntschli with her heroic but condescending gesture in order to prove to him that she's braver than he.

Bluntschli — to confess to Raina that the pistol is empty, in order to put her even more at ease so she won't fear and therefore betray him.

CC:

Trigger: Bluntschli admits that he's so unsoldierly as to carry chocolate instead of bullets.

Heap: Bluntschli's confession outrages Raina's romantic ideals.

36

Raina — to throw a bone to a contemptible beggar (Bluntschli) in order to prove that her romantic ideals make her superior to Bluntschli.

Bluntschli — to flatter Raina into feeding him in order to gorge. Reminded by the mention of chocolate, Bluntschli is pierced by hunger. He begins regressing to his child self

CC:

Trigger: Grossed out by Bluntschli's despicable bad manners, Raina grabs the box away from him.

Heap: Frightened again, Bluntschli complains.

35

	I am sorry I frightened you. (*She takes up the pistol and hands it to him.*) Pray take it to protect yourself against me.
The Man	(*Grinning wearily at the sarcasm as he takes the pistol*) No use, dear young lady: there's nothing in it. It's not loaded. (*He makes a grimace at it, and drops it disparagingly into his revolver case.*)
Raina	Load it by all means.
The Man	I've no ammunition. What use are cartridges in battle? I always carry chocolate <u>instead; and I finished the last cake of that hours ago.</u>

36

Raina	(*Outraged in her most cherished ideals of manhood.*) Chocolate! Do you stuff your pockets with sweets — like a schoolboy — even in the field?
The Man	(*Grinning*) Yes: isn't it contemptible? (Hungrily) I wish I had some now.
Raina	Allow me. (*she sails away scornfully to the chest of drawers, and returns with the box of confectionery in her hand.*) I am sorry I have eaten them all except these. (*She offers him the box.*)
The Man	(*Ravenously*) You're an angel! (*He gobbles the contents.*) Creams! Delicious! (*He looks anxiously to see whether there are any more. There are none: he can only scrape the box with his fingers and suck them. When that nourishment is exhausted he accepts the inevitable with pathetic good humor, and says, with grateful emotion*) Bless you, dear lady! You can always tell an old soldier by the insides of his holsters and cartridge boxes. The young ones carry pistols and cartridges: the old ones grub. Thank you. (*He hands back the box. <u>She snatches it contemptuously from him and throws it away. He shies again, as if she had</u> <u>meant to strike him.)</u>*

37

Bluntschli — to confess his weakness to Raina in order to make her feel sorry for him, like a child calling for its mother. Bluntschli continues to regress to his childhood self. Fear, fatigue, and hunger make him vulnerable

Raina — to mock Bluntschli's weakness in order to flatter herself with her superiority

CC:

Trigger: Bluntschli's childlike vulnerability touches Raina's maternal instincts.

Heap: Raina reaches out to console Bluntschli.

38

Bluntschli — to seek nurturing from Raina in order to touch her heart

Raina — to mother Bluntschli in order to rescue a soul who needs her.

CC: **Important:** There is a moment of attraction, of sexual tension, between Raina and Bluntschli. Raina, sensitive to issues of propriety, quickly breaks the moment and withdraws.

Trigger: Raina is shocked by the sudden attraction she feels to Bluntschli; she's an engaged woman!!

Heap: Raina backs off and pretends nothing happened.

37

	Ugh! Don't do things so suddenly, gracious lady. It's mean to revenge yourself because I frightened you just now.
Raina	(*Loftily*) Frighten me! Do you know, sir, that though I am only a woman, I think I am at heart as brave as you.
The Man	I should think so. You haven't been under fire for three days as I have. I can stand two days without showing it much; but no man can stand three days: I'm as nervous as a mouse. (*He sits down on the ottoman, and takes his head in his hands.*) Would you like to see me cry?
Raina	(*Alarmed*) No.
The Man	If you would, all you have to do is to scold me just as if I were a little boy and you my <u>nurse. If I were in camp now, they'd play all sorts of tricks on me.</u>

38

Raina	(*A little moved*) I'm sorry. I won't scold you. (*Touched by the sympathy in her tone, <u>he raises his head and looks gratefully at her;</u>*)

39

Raina — to put Bluntschli down in order to disguise her attraction to him. The moment of connection has unsettled her, so she retreats into her idealism.

Bluntschli — to criticize the enemy soldiers for lack of professionalism in order to disguise his attraction to Raina. The moment of connection has unsettled him, so he retreats into his professionalism.

CC:

Trigger: Bluntschli's critique of the cavalry charge reminds Raina of her dreams of military glory.

Heap: Raina presses Bluntschli for the story. Power reversal.

40

Raina — to beg Bluntschli for the tale, like a child for a bedtime story, in order to wrap herself in her cloak of ideals and worship her hero.

Bluntschli — to instruct the naïve child in order to take charge of the situation.

CC:

Trigger: Bluntschli criticizes the soldier leading the charge.

Heap: Bluntschli's critique of a "hero" (like Sergius) arouses Raina's defensiveness, and she protests.

39

	she immediately draws back and says stiffly) You must excuse me; our soldiers are not like that. (*She moves away from the ottoman.*)
The Man	Oh yes they are. There are only two sorts of soldiers; old ones and young ones. I've served fourteen years; half of your fellows never smelt powder before. Why how is it that you've just beaten us? Sheer ignorance of the art of war, nothing else. (*Indignantly*) I never saw anything so unprofessional.
Raina	(*Ironically*) Oh! Was it unprofessional to beat you?
The Man	Well, come! Is it professional to throw a regiment of cavalry on a battery of machine guns, with the dead certainty that if the guns go off not a horse or man will ever get within fifty yards of the fire? <u>I couldn't believe my eyes when I saw it.</u>

40

Raina	(*Eagerly turning to him, as all her enthusiasms and her dreams of glory rush back on her*) Did you see the great cavalry charge? Oh, tell me about it. Describe it to me.
The Man	You never saw a cavalry charge, did you?
Raina	How could I?
The Man	Ah, perhaps not. No: of course not! Well, it's a funny sight. It's like slinging a handful of peas against a windowpane: first one comes; then two or three close behind him; and then all the rest in a lump.
Raina	(*Her eyes dilating as she raises her clasped hands ecstatically*) Yes, first One! The bravest ofthe brave!
The Man	<u>(*prosaically*) Hm! You should see the poor devil pulling at his horse.</u>

41

Bluntschli — to unmask Raina's illusions in order to justify himself.

Raina — to protest Bluntschli's unromantic view of things in order to cling to her ideals.

CC:

Trigger: Bluntschli agrees that the leader of today's charge looked like a hero.

Heap: Since he seems to be conceding that she's right, Raina forgives his cynicism and pleads for details.

41

Raina	Why should he pull at his horse?
The Man	(*Impatient of so stupid a question*) It's running away with him, of course: do you suppose the fellow wants to get there before the others and be killed? Then they all come. You can tell the young ones by their wildness and their slashing. The old ones come bunched up under the number one guard: they know that they're mere projectiles, and that it's no use trying to fight. The wounds are mostly broken knees, from the horses cannoning together.
Raina	Ugh! But I don't believe the first man is a coward. I know he is a hero!
The Man	(*Good humoredly*) That's what you'd have said if you'd seen the first man in the charge today.

42

Bluntschli — to mock the romantic folly of the leader of the charge in order to prove to Raina his view of war is right. Bluntschli sets Raina up, only to knock her down. He thinks he's telling a great joke. The dramatic irony is that he doesn't know he's talking about Raina's fiancé.

Raina — to mask her shock and horror from Bluntschli in order to cling to her ideals as long as she can.

CC:

Trigger: Bluntschli's depiction of Sergius as a fool wounds Raina deeply, striking at the heart of her Romantic ideals

Heap: Raina plots revenge.

43

Raina — to confront and humiliate Bluntschli in order to take revenge on him.

Bluntschli — to impress Raina with his attentiveness to her in order to flatter her into giving him more treats. He's like a bird dog "on point," tense with anticipation.

CC:

Trigger: Raina confronts Bluntschli with the portrait.

Heap: Bluntschli recognizes the portrait and realizes his goof.

42

Raina	(*Breathless, forgiving him everything*) Ah, I knew it! Tell me. Tell me about him.
The Man	He did it like an operatic tenor. A regular handsome fellow, with flashing eyes and lovely moustache, shouting his war-cry and charging like Don Quixote at the windmills. We did laugh.
Raina	You dare to laugh!
The Man	Yes, but when the sergeant ran up as white as a sheet, and told us they'd sent us the wrong ammunition, and that we couldn't fire a round for the next ten minutes, we laughed out the other side of our mouths. I never felt so sick in my life; though I've been in one or two very tight places. And I hadn't even a revolver cartridge: only chocolate. We'd no bayonets: nothing. Of course, they just cut us to bits. And there was Don Quixote flourishing like a drum major, thinking he'd done the cleverest thing ever known, whereas he ought to be court-martialed for it. Of all the fools ever let loose on the field of battle, that man must be the very maddest. <u>He and his regiment simply committed suicide; only the pistol missed fire; that's all.</u>

43

Raina	(*Deeply wounded, but steadfastly loyal to her ideals*) Indeed! Would you know him again if you saw him?
The Man	Shall I ever forget him!
Raina	(*She again goes to the chest of drawers. He watches her with a vague hope that she may have something more for him to eat. She takes the portrait from its stand and brings it to <u>him.</u>)* <u>That is a photograph of the gentleman — the patriot and hero — to whom I am betrothed.</u>

44

Bluntschli — to apologize to Raina in order to try to stifle his laughter. Bluntschli realizes his mistake, but he's struck with the humor of the situation and can't hold his laughter in.

Raina — to probe Bluntschli in order to threaten him not to laugh at her. She's furious with him.

CC:

Trigger: Bluntschli just can't stop laughing.

Heap: His laughter offends and wounds Raina even further.

45

Raina — to dramatize her ideals to make Bluntschli feel guilty

Bluntschli — to rationalize Sergius's behavior in order to try to make up to Raina for his mistake. He just makes things worse.

CC:

Trigger: Shots ring out, reminding them both of the hovering danger — and that Raina holds the power of life and death over Bluntschli.

Heap: Raina takes advantage of her power to punish Bluntschli.

44

The Man	(*Recognizing it with a shock*) I'm really very sorry. (*Looking at her*) Was it fair to lead me on? (*He looks at the portrait again.*) Yes: that's Don Quixote: not a doubt of it. (*He stifles a laugh.*)
Raina	(*Quickly*) Why do you laugh?
The Man	(*Apologetic, but still greatly tickled*) I didn't laugh, I assure you. At least I didn't mean to. But when I think of him charging the windmills and imagining he was doing the finest <u>thing — (He chokes with suppressed laughter.)</u>

45

Raina	(*Sternly*) Give me back the portrait, Sir.
The Man	(*With sincere remorse*) Of course. Certainly. I'm really very sorry. (*He hands her the picture. She deliberately kisses it and looks him straight in the face before returning to the chest of drawers to replace it. He follows her, apologizing.*) Perhaps I'm quite wrong, you know: no doubt I am. Most likely he had got wind of the cartridge business somehow, and knew it was a safe job.
Raina	That is to say, he was a pretender and a coward! You did not dare say that before.
The Man	(*With a comic gesture of despair*) It's no use, dear lady: I can't make you see it from the professional point of view. (*As he turns away to get back to the ottoman,* <u>a **couple of distant shots** threaten renewed trouble.</u>)

What are the criteria for scenic units?

Criteria for Objectives

1. Verb choices must meet all the criteria for actable verbs.
2. Tactic objective verbs must be transitive.
3. Every character onstage during a unit must have an objective, whether or not that character speaks in the unit. Verbs such as "to listen" are too weak.
4. Tactic objective must clearly identify how the character goes about achieving his/her goal in this unit.
5. Goal objective must clearly identify at a psychological level what the character wants to do in this unit.

Criteria for Cause of Change

1. Both trigger and heap must be identified clearly.
2. Choices of trigger and heap should show psychological insight into characters.
3. It must be clear how trigger causes heap.
4. It must be clear how CC causes a change in tactical pattern.
5. CC must lead into the following unit.

Criteria for Where to Divide Units

1. Divisions must be clearly defined and analysis of unit matched to unit in scene.
2. Choice of where to divide should show psychological insight.
3. In general, units should be of appropriate length to capture the tactical patterns in the scene, neither too small nor too large

Criteria for Format

1. Format should be *exactly* the same as the format used in the *Arms and the Man* example. This format is not only efficient; it is standard in the industry. Presentation should be neat and legible.

Capstone Assigment: Scenic Units

Part A: Analysis
For this assignment, use the script you analyzed in the previous chapter. Imagine that you, the actor, are preparing to play the

character for which you created spines. If you have not yet developed character spines, do so as preparation for the exercise below.

1. Choose a short two-character scene from the script, one in which your character appears for a substantial period of time. If your instructor approves, the class might work in pairs: you could partner with a classmate who wrote spines for the other character who appears in the scene. Partners could share the character analysis they did, including spines. Each student individually would then write his own unit analysis.
2. Write a unit analysis of the scene, using the format demonstrated in the *Arms and the Man* example, pp. 101-118.
3. Draw on the analysis of the script's given circumstances you developed when creating your spines. You would find it helpful to do structural analysis of the script, and — if you're not working with a partner — character analysis of the other character in the scene. If you don't understand a character, you won't know what she wants and how she goes about getting it.
4. Use the criteria for writing scenic units to guide your thinking.
5. Give yourself plenty of time to complete this project. Unit analysis is hard work and extremely time-consuming!

Part B: Mental Management: Reflection

1. What specific goal did you set for yourself when you began work on this assignment?
2. What for you seemed the biggest obstacle in the way of your achieving your goal?
3. What strategies did you use to try to overcome the obstacle?
4. Which strategies worked best? Why?

Peer Review Checklists for Capstone Assignments can be found in Appendix B.

Chapter 7
Thematic Statements

EXERCISE 7:1
What does "meaning" mean?

1. Think of a significant experience that changed your understanding about something or someone.
2. Describe what happened, what you thought, and what you felt.
3. What did the experience mean to you? What made it significant?
4. What makes something meaningful to you?

Did you know current brain science shows that emotional involvement is a key ingredient in making experience meaningful? A theatrical performance strives to stimulate both mind and emotions so audiences and artists may share a "virtual experience" which can convey new insights about significant patterns in human life. In order for theatre artists to create such an experience, however, they have to figure out what the story *means*.

Figuring out what a script means requires us to use the tools we've learned. We must analyze the given circumstances, structure, and characters. We may have intuitive ideas after reading the script once, but if we're going to produce it, we need more than intuition. We need to dig deeper and read closely to develop a thematic statement.

What is a thematic statement?

A **thematic statement** (**TS**) describes your interpretation of the story's meaning. What do you think the playwright is showing us about the human experience? Thematic statements identify what you think the playwright is communicating about a specific **thematic subject (TSub)**. Artistic collaborators use thematic statements to enrich their pre-production discussions.

The thematic statement has a specific format with three parts: identification of the script and playwright, identification of a thematic subject, *and* an interpretation of what the story shows you about the subject. Sometimes people confuse thematic statement with thematic subject so let's take a closer look at those two parts.

Thematic subjects are issues the script explores. They are not expressed as complete sentences. In literature classes, you may have identified issues such as "women's rights," "alienation, "or "young love" as **themes** found in literature. Here we are working deeply with a single script. Identifying an issue, a thematic subject, is the first step to writing a thematic statement. However, the statement is not complete without including the theatrical artist's point of view about that subject *in the form of a complete sentence.*

Think of thematic subjects as threads woven together to create the fabric of the story; one story contains many subject threads. By clearly articulating a thematic statement you are choosing one subject, one thread, you want to bring to the audience's attention. Think of your chosen subject/thread as made of gold and the other subject/threads as made of grey cotton. You can create patterns in performance to help the audience see your chosen thematic subject just as you can create patterns in fabric to foreground your gold thread. The particular pattern you weave represents the complete thematic statement, your particular interpretation of the thematic subject.

Example 7:1 The Structure of a Thematic Statement

Consider the following thematic statement:

"In *Arms and the Man*, Shaw shows **that** when it comes to love and war, we're all children."

If we dissect the statement to discover its component parts we have:

Identification of the **script and playwright**: *Arms and the Man,* by Shaw

Identification of a **thematic subject**: "love and war."

Explanation of your **point of view**: "We're all children [in matters of love and war].

The second and third part, following "that" in the statement, form an independent clause. In other words, if you remove "that," the second and third parts together can stand on their own as a complete sentence, e.g., "When it comes to love and war, we're all children." Make sure you have a complete sentence following "that." If you don't, you don't have a complete thematic statement.

Where do I find clues to help me develop my thematic statement?

There are five major sources of clues to a script's meaning: **the main action, patterns in the script, the script's title, any philosophical statements made** by characters, and **contradictions and structural oddities.**

1. **The Main Action**

   The main action is the most significant source of meaning and thus the best clue to the *thematic statement*. Two previously explored tools reveal the script's *main action: structural analysis* and the *RAS*.

   a. *Structural Analysis* and the *RAS* help you discern the script's thematic subjects and the playwright's view about those subjects. The major crisis and major structural climax provide particularly important clues. After completing your RAS and structural analysis ask yourself the following questions:
      - What kind of person (protagonist) takes this action?
      - What kind of action does the person take?
      - What happens to the protagonist as a result of the action?
      - What discovery does the protagonist make at the major crisis?
      - How does the discovery lead to the major structural climax?

   b. The root action statement only helps you articulate a thematic statement if it transcends story level. A story level RAS yields a story level thematic statement. Let's look at a series of paired RASes and resulting thematic statements for *Oedipus the King*. In the examples below, we critique the thematic statement that grew out of each RAS. Look closely, as each succeeding pair represents a step away from story level and towards the philosophical level.

Example 7:2 Clues In the RAS

- **DRAFT A:**

  RAS: "*Oedipus the King* is about a clever man who searches for the killer of the previous king only to discover that he himself is the murderer, so he punishes himself."

  TS: "In *Oedipus the King*, Sophocles shows that crime doesn't pay."

  Evaluation of TS:
  - Correct format
  - Justifiable on the basis of what happens in the script
  - It's cliché
  - It's too general, could apply to multiple scripts
  - Does not include important ideas and images included in the script
  - It is boring — does not stimulate creativity

- **DRAFT B:**

  RAS: "*Oedipus the King* is about a stubborn man who attempts to escape his fate, but when he discovers he has unknowingly fulfilled his destiny, he surrenders to the gods."

  TS: "In *Oedipus the King*, Sophocles shows that human life is ruled by fate."

  Evaluation of TS
  - Correct format
  - Justifiable on the basis of what happens in the script
  - Justifiable on the basis of some philosophical statements in the dialogue
  - Not a cliché
  - Includes some important ideas in the script, expanding upon TSub in RAS
  - Is a significant statement about human life but perhaps could be more profound if RAS were more insightful
  - Is more likely to stimulate artistic creativity than Example A

- **DRAFT C:**

<u>RAS</u>: "*Oedipus the King* is about a willful, spiritually blind man who seeks to wrest the truth from life with his intelligence, but when he discovers life is ruled by fate, he surrenders to the gods, trading physical sight for spiritual insight."

<u>TS</u>: "In *Oedipus the King*, Sophocles shows that intelligence alone does not allow a person to discover his/her purpose in life: to the contrary, one must develop spiritual insight and trust in the cosmic forces to lead one along the path of one's destiny."

<u>Evaluation of TS</u>:
  - Correct format
  - Justifiable on the basis of what happens in the script, as well as an important pattern of imagery
  - Not a cliché
  - A significant interpretation of the meaning of some aspect of human life, with deeper understanding than example B
  - Stimulates artistic creativity

One could certainly find additional thematic statements for *Oedipus the King*. There is no one "right" thematic statement for any story. However, some thematic statements are more effective than others at stimulating artistic creativity and personal insight into the narrative.

1. Read the story below.

> **EXERCISE 7:2**
> Your turn!

The Dragon That Munched
By Suzanne Burgoyne

"Roger!" his mother called up the stairs. "Have you finished your homework?"

"I wish," said Roger to Dragon, "there was no such word as homework."

Actually, Roger didn't say that. He typed it on Dragon's keyboard. Dragon was a computer. A new, hush-hush, experimental model computer that Roger's dad (a very important scientist) was working on. Roger wasn't supposed to be playing with Dragon, of course. But his friend Charlie was a computer whiz, so Roger needed to practice to keep up.

The prompt DO NEXT? appeared in green letters on Dragon's monitor.

Roger was getting a headache from concentrating so hard. Also, he was hungry.

EAT, he typed.

EAT WHAT? replied Dragon.

COOKIE, typed Roger.

YUM, printed Dragon. THANK YOU.

Roger turned off Dragon and went down to the kitchen. "Mom," he said, "may I have a nibble-fritz?"

"What?" said his mother.

"I said, I'd like a chompsickle."

"What?"

No matter how hard Roger tried, he couldn't say the word cookie. Finally, he drew a picture.

"Ah," said Mother, "I know what you want." She handed him an orange.

Roger was hungry, so he ate the orange. Actually, it tasted pretty good. But it wasn't a cookie.

Roger went back upstairs to Dragon.

He typed, DID YOU EAT THE WORD — Roger discovered he couldn't type cookie, either — NUMMIEWAT?

YUM, printed Dragon. EAT NEXT?

Roger thought for a moment. Slowly, he typed into the computer, HOMEWORK.

YUM, said Dragon. EAT NEXT?

"Roger!" his mother called up the stairs. "Have you finished your thinkdoodle?"

"I'm doing it now, Mom," he yelled. He went to the phone and called his friend Charlie.

"Hey, Charlie, what are you doing?" "I'm doing my memorpickle."

"That's what I thought," said Roger. "It can wait. Come over here. I've got something to show you."

Since Charlie lived next door, it wasn't long before he was standing next to Roger, blinking at Dragon's screen. "A computer that eats words? And after Dragon eats a word, nobody can say it? Hmm," he muttered. "There are number-crunching programs. But a program that munches words is something new. What are you going to do?" "Well," said Roger, "I was thinking of all the words I could feed to Dragon. Words I'd like to get rid of, like 'karate lessons.' I mean, my parents couldn't make me go if they couldn't say it, right?"

"I see what you mean," Charlie said. "But your vision is limited. Think big."

Before Roger could stop him, Charlie leaned over and typed NUCLEAR MISSILE after Dragon's EAT NEXT? prompt.

YUM, said Dragon. THANK YOU. EAT NEXT?

"Was that such a good idea?" asked Roger.

For some reason Roger wasn't very hungry for supper that night.

"Would you like a tumtickle for dessert?" his mother asked.

Roger shook his head. He hurried to wash the dishes so he could watch the evening news.

"And the crisis of the hour, "the newscaster was saying, "is the breakdown in the arms negotiation talks. At the special session tonight, negotiators on both sides found themselves unable to pronounce the words bumbledy boomdoom."

Onto the screen flashed a frenzied scene. Men and women in dark suits shook their fists at one another across a long table.

Roger ran to the phone. "Charlie," he whispered, "get over here. Fast. We're in trouble."

Roger waited for Charlie to arrive before switching on Dragon.

HELLO, flashed Dragon's screen. EAT NEXT?

"What do we do?" Roger demanded. "We've got to get him to give the words back."

Another EAT NEXT? Prompt flashed impatiently on the screen.

"Greedy, isn't it?" observed Charlie.

Suddenly Roger sat down at the keyboard and began typing.

"What are you doing?" Charlie asked.

CHOCOLATE FUDGE CAKE, typed Roger frantically, PISTACHIO ICE CREAM. LICORICE STICKS.

"Stop!" cried Charlie. "Not ticklish fix!"

YUM, printed Dragon. YUM. YUM.

ROOT BEER FLOAT, Roger typed. PEANUT-BUTTER-AND-JELLY SANDWICH. BUTTERED POPCORN.

YUM, YUM, YUM, said Dragon.

Charlie collapsed, blinking, into a chair. Roger's fingers were sweaty on the keyboard. He sure hoped this would work.

BANANA SPLIT. COCONUT DOUGHNUT. PIZZA WITH ANCHOVIES.

YUM, printed Dragon. YUM. All at once his letters flickered, like a hiccup. YUK.

Dragon's monitor suddenly filled with words, spewing across the screen faster than Roger could read them. Roger took a deep breath and crossed his fingers. "Cookie," he said.

"How did you do that?" Charlie asked.

Roger shrugged. "I just remembered what happened to me one time when I ate a lot of that stuff."

"You made Dragon upchuck all the words? By feeding him all that stuff?" Charlie blinked in disgust. "Yuk."

"Roger!" his mother called up the stairs. "Have you finished your homework?"

Roger thought those were the most wonderful words he'd ever heard.

Story reprinted from the July-August 1986 issue of Highlights for Children *by permission of* Highlights for Children, Inc.

2. Write an RAS for the story.
3. Use the criteria for writing a good RAS to guide your work.
4. Take the RAS through several drafts until it's unified and you have an RAS that transcends story level.
5. Identify a thematic subject from the story.
6. Following the process in Example 7:2 above, create a thematic statement that includes the thematic subject you

have identified and pairs effectively with the main action articulated in your RAS.

7. Take the pairs through several drafts using the evaluation process for each pair outlined above.

EXERCISE 7:3
One more time

1. Repeat the exercise above. When you get to step 5, identify a different thematic subject.
2. Continue through the rest of the exercise.
3. Compare the final thematic statements from each exercise.
4. Which one best reflects your interpretation of the story?
5. Why?

2. **Patterns In the Script**

Recognizing patterns is an essential process in human thinking. Indeed, if we couldn't perceive patterns in the multitudinous impressions bombarding our senses, our world would be totally chaotic. In order to search for meaning in any subject, we look for patterns.

Sometimes by using real-life patterns as a lens through which to view a script, we can gain new insights. Fascinating patterns abound in our world, if we're perceptive enough to notice them. For instance, if you read or saw *The Da Vinci Code*, you may remember the Fibonacci Sequence, which served as a clue. The sequence begins as follows:

1, 1, 2, 3, 5, 8, 13, 21, 34, 55, 89 …

What is the mathematical pattern Fibonacci discovered?

Figure 7:1
Fibonacci patterns in nature: a sunflower disk.

As Marcia Birken and Anne Coon demonstrate in *Discovering Patterns in Mathematics and Poetry*, the Fibonacci Numbers appear frequently in nature. For instance, in the disks of daisies and sunflowers, you find at least two sets of spirals, one going clockwise and the other counter-clockwise. If you count each set of spirals, you'll see they usually "just happen" to be consecutive Fibonacci numbers. The same phenomenon appears in the spirals of objects such as pineapples, pinecones, and artichokes. Can you see the spirals in the center of the sunflower in Fig. 7.1? Can you count the number of spirals in each direction?

We began this chapter by stating that the experience of see-ing/doing a play "can convey new insights about significant patterns in human life." A script contains multiple kinds of patterns that, when recognized, can help identify a significant thematic thread. The tools with which we've already been working require us to identify patterns. For instance, our structural analysis results from recognizing a pattern of ac-tions that create a rising tide of tension. We have also learned to recognize a smaller pattern of triggers and heaps within scenes that leads to changes in a character's tactics. Now we are going to look at patterns in the script that help us inter-pret the story's meaning.

a. Patterns of **Imagery.**

Images in scripts communicate meaning at deeper levels of consciousness. In *Oedipus the King*, for example, we can identify a pattern of sight and blindness. The physically blind prophet Tiresias "sees" things that Oedipus, an intelligent man with physical sight, cannot see. Tiresias "sees" Oedipus has fulfilled the prophecy, but Oedipus cannot "hear" Tiresias's truth. When Oedipus learns he has killed his father and married his mother, he blinds himself. Sophocles associates images of sight and blindness with issues about the ability to perceive truth. A thematic statement based on imagery patterns might look like this: "In *Oedipus the King*, Sophocles shows that human intellect and the physical senses don't allow us to discover the truth about how the universe works; instead, we need spiritual insight to understand life's mysteries."

Close examination of imagery in a script can uncover clues to its meaning. Ask yourself the following questions in reference to imagery:
- Are there repeated images in the script?
- With what characters are those images associated?
- With what actions are those images associated?
- With what ideas are those images associated?
- Does the pattern of images evolve as the script progresses?

b. Patterns of **Human Experience.**

Thematic analysis may begin with a search for an essential pattern of human experience embedded in the action of the story. Two universal patterns in human life involve 1) *change,* 2) *learning.* Most scripts dramatize one or both. It is always helpful to ask yourself: What changes during the script? What does the protagonist learn (or fail to learn)?

A variant on change and learning is *initiation.* The transformation of human identity recurs so often in life that we have created initiation rituals to enable it. Such patterns range from a native going on a vision quest to a graduation ceremony marking a change from youth to adulthood.

Other basic patterns include:
- *The hero's journey,* in which the hero is on a quest for some valuable object. This pattern usually shows the hero passing through a series of tests to prove his/her worthiness.
- *The rise to or fall from power,* in which causes of success and failure are explored.
- *The battle between good and evil,* which does not always end with the "good guys" winning.
- *The departure from and/or return to home.*
- *The pattern of the cycles of human life and/or the seasons.* These patterns may go so far as to examine a soul's journey from birth to death.

Patterns may overlap and any given script may be viewed through the lens of more than one type of pattern.

1. Make a list of all the basic patterns of human existence you can imagine.

EXERCISE 7:4
What patterns do you know?

2. Can you think of a film, script, or story that exemplifies each pattern?

3. In your interpretation, which pattern best fits the script for which you did your RAS analysis?

Example 7:3 Using Patterns of Human Experience to Think Through *Avatar* Thematic Analysis

Let's see how an experienced script analyst works through an example of pattern analysis for the film *Avatar*.

- **Analysis: Thematic Subject #1** I start by thinking about the thematic ideas I considered when writing my RAS. The first thematic subject that struck me when I walked out of the movie theatre is "environmentalism." The film seems strongly to support saving Pandora from the greedy corporation. By analogy Pandora could refer to Earth. Jake proclaims no speck of living green can be found on the sky people's planet: Earthmen have "killed their mother."

- **Interpretation: Pattern Recognition** This topic seems related to the paradigm shift Jake undergoes at the major crisis. He learns that his own race is "evil," and the Na'vi are "good." So the film fits the pattern of *the battle between good and evil.*

- **Creating Thematic Statement #1** "In *Avatar,* James Cameron shows that corporate greed must be opposed by 'the people' to avert catastrophic destruction of nature."

- **Evaluation** I get this message strongly from the film, which, at this point, I think is making a political statement. It's a complicated film however, and here I'm starting with the most obvious interpretation.

- **Analysis: Thematic Subject #2** A second thematic subject is "wholeness." Jake has lost a part of himself in a war. The avatar body gives him legs, thus wholeness. However he could regain the use of his human legs by fulfilling the Colonel's orders. He has to choose which path to wholeness he wants to take.

- **Interpretation: Pattern Recognition** Again, this subject leads me to consider the pattern of *the battle between good and evil.* Jake has to choose between good and evil ways of becoming whole.

- **Creating Thematic Statement #2** "In *Avatar,* James Cameron

shows that it is better to choose good than to choose evil."
- **Evaluation** This interpretation isn't insightful. The thematic statement is cliché. I need to think more about the significance of "wholeness." Is "wholeness" a symbol for something that's more than physical?
- **Going Deeper** If we abstract up a level, Jake's physical loss may symbolize a greater loss: alienation from a spiritual unity represented by Pandora's network of energy connecting all living things. The basic pattern this idea suggests is *the hero's journey.* The protagonist goes on a quest to find his lost wholeness.
- **Creating Thematic Statement #3** "In *Avatar,* James Cameron shows that contemporary humans have lost our spiritual connection to the unity of life, including nature, and must embark on a quest to seek that lost connection."
- **Evaluation** I'm excited! I think I'm on the track of something! I need to go further; the statement doesn't capture the entire meaning of the film. Back to analysis!
- **Analysis: Thematic Subject #3** A third meaning of the film relates to "transformation." An avatar can be interpreted as a metaphor for transformation of identity. In the *initiation* pattern, a ritual provides a process through which a person changes identity, often undergoing symbolic death and rebirth. I think about all the religious ceremonies in *Avatar.* The film begins with a symbolic death and rebirth as Jake replaces his twin brother. It ends in a literal death and rebirth in which the human form of Jake dies so he can be reborn as a Na'vi.
- **Creating Thematic Statement #4** "In *Avatar,* James Cameron shows that one must undergo an initiation rite including death and rebirth in order to transform into a spiritual being with a connection to the universal whole."
- **Evaluation** I'm inspired by these ideas, too! I've now developed four possible thematic statements for *Avatar.* The second I've discarded because it's a cliché. The first has value but it is too obvious. The third and fourth seem useful but incomplete.
- **Mental Management** In order to progress further, I next revisit the draft of my RAS from the last chapter. I could have started my analysis with the RAS, but I was struggling to find

a comprehensive thematic statement and wanted to see if the "pattern of human experience" approach would clarify my thinking.

- **Synthesizing the RAS with the Thematic Statement** RAS *Avatar* draft #7: "This script is about a crippled warrior who seeks wholeness by pretending to transform into a member of a 'primitive' culture, but when he discovers his own race is evil and the natives are part of a planetary spiritual whole, he proves his worthiness and transforms for real."

- **Evaluation** As I look at my description of the protagonist, I wonder if "warrior" is necessary. Is it crucial to my interpretation of the meaning of the film that Jake is a Marine? Does the film's meaning only apply to soldiers? I want to re-think the first part of my RAS. The great battle Jake leads certainly takes up a great deal of time in the film. A thematic statement could be developed that focuses on war. For instance, Jake mentions that the soldiers on earth are fighting for freedom, while the soldiers on Pandora are mere mercenaries who've sold their skills to the corporation.

- **Creating Thematic Statement #5** "In *Avatar,* James Cameron shows that fighting for freedom is heroic, but fighting to support corporate greed is evil"

- **Evaluation** The film could support this interpretation, though the interpretation would leave out many significant events. Why do I choose not to emphasize war in my analysis? I need to acknowledge my personal biases: I'm not a fan of war and violence. I prefer peaceful solutions. I let myself off the hook by considering Jake's leading the Na'vi defense as one of the tests he undergoes in the hero's journey aspect of the "proving his worthiness" part of the RAS.

- **Synthesizing the RAS with the Thematic Statement** RAS *Avatar* draft # 8: "This script is about a crippled *soul* who seeks wholeness by pretending to transform into a member of a 'primitive' culture, but when he discovers his own race is evil and the natives are part of a planetary spiritual whole, he proves his worthiness and transforms for real."

- **Evaluation** Again, the paradigm shift strikes me as crucial.

The loss and rediscovery of spiritual wholeness appears in two of my thematic statements. I may want to re-word the major crisis in order to emphasize the significance of the paradigm shift.

- **Synthesizing the RAS with the Thematic Statement** RAS *Avatar* draft # 9: "This script is about a crippled soul who seeks wholeness by pretending to transform into a member of a *savage* culture, but when he discovers his own race *are the savages* and the natives connected to a spiritual whole, he proves his worthiness and transforms for real."

- **Evaluation** Transformation seems to be so central to the story that it must have an important role in the film's meaning. This RAS emphasizes transformation.

- **Going Deeper** The RAS section that I am having difficulty understanding thematically is the main action itself. What is the relationship between Jake's pretending to be a Na'vi, his paradigm shift, and his choice to become a Na'vi in reality? What does it mean that Jake pretends to transform into a Na'vi? What does the symbol of the avatar represent in the main action?

Thinking … thinking … Hmm. One of the things the corporate colonizers lost is the ability to experience the natural world directly, through their senses. They live isolated, inside an environment created by technology. They strut through the world encased in huge machines. They no longer value the living beings they have shut out of their experience. The Colonel refers to the Na'vi as "cockroaches."

If I compare the avatar body with the machine the Colonel operates, I see that the avatar body allows Jake to experience the world though nature, the spiritual world. He can bond with other beings and the deity herself. He can train his avatar body to accomplish heroic deeds. He enjoys the feeling of flying, connected to the ikran.

However, Jake needs help to understand his new experiences. There is a symbolic pattern in the film related to "seeing." Grace tells Jake he must learn to see the world through Neytiri's eyes. Early in the film Neytiri and other Na'vi say that Jake can't "see." The greeting, "I see you," has special meaning. In the Na'vi culture, it means perceiving a person's spirit behind the eyes. Jake and Neytiri do not use this greeting with each other until after Jake's paradigm shift. Neytiri later tells Jake she "sees" him even though he is currently in his human body. The final frame of the film is a close-up on Jake's new eyes, confirming the completion of his transformation.

Consider also that the theme song for the film is entitled "I See You."

The theme song lyrics include lines about learning to see the world anew with the help of one's lover. In order to reach his paradigm shift, Jake has to change his way of seeing.

- **Interpretation** So the main action of the film, plus the symbolic pattern of "seeing" imply that only through learning to see the world through the eyes of the *whole* person can we break through cultural conditioning and discover the unity of life. Neytiri teaches Jake to attune himself to nature and connect to the tree of souls. The main action is complex because it describes an action that begins as deceit but becomes an initiation, a spiritual training.

- **Creating Thematic Statement #6** "In *Avatar,* James Cameron shows that twenty-first century humans have lost our connections to nature and become greedy, mechanized monsters that destroy all they touch, but if we can learn to see how everything is connected, we can die as materialistic selves and be reborn as spiritual beings, restoring our connections with each other and the cosmic whole."

- **Creating Thematic Statement #7** "In *Avatar,* James Cameron shows that 'civilized' humans have lost our spiritual connections and become greedy, materialistic monsters, but if we can walk a mile in the moccasins of a 'whole' being and see the natural world through uncluttered eyes, we can shed our corrupted egos and transform into spiritual beings, restoring our connections with all life and the cosmic whole."

- **Evaluation** I now have two possible thematic statements. Both are complex. I like some aspects of each, but I am not entirely satisfied with either. However, both are supported by evidence from the film, including the main action and an important pattern of symbols. The patterns of human behavior I examined helped me explore some universal ideas arising from the main action.

- **Summary** Notice that as I delved into the meaning of the film, I also made revisions to my RAS. The RAS and the thematic statement are closely intertwined so that change in one often suggests change in the other. Furthermore, all of the script analysis tools can give us insights to use in another area of analysis. The more you practice using the tools, the more ideas generated by thinking about spines, for example, will inspire new perceptions about structure or thematic statement, and vice versa. Instead of a linear step-by-step process, the analysis will transform into a web of interweaving discoveries — perhaps resembling the energy web of the planet Pandora in *Avatar*?

3. **Title of Script**
   A title does more than just give a script a name. For instance, the title of Henrik Ibsen's script *A Doll's House* suggests the protagonist is a doll, a toy for her husband's enjoyment, rather than a person in her own right. Consider the following questions when looking at a script's title:
   - Is there an image or metaphor in the title?
   - Does the title give a hint about the meaning?

   1. Make a list of the titles of scripts and films you know well.
   2. Which titles give clues to the script's meaning?
   3. How do those titles help you understand the theme?

   EXERCISE 7:5
   Do you know titles that give clues to meaning?

4. **Philosophical Statements by Characters In the Script**
   In their dialogue, characters can reveal the playwright's point of view about thematic subjects. Sometimes a character functions specifically as the playwright's voice. This type of character, most frequently found in period pieces, is called a **raisonneur**, the voice of reason. In modern scripts, several characters might share this function. Sometimes, though not in all scripts, a character speaks a line of dialogue that could be a thematic statement. Let's look at a familiar film to see how this approach works.

In *Harry Potter and the Chamber of Secrets*, Harry's story level main action is to solve the mystery of the Chamber. All kinds of hints embedded in the script, however, show that at a philosophical level, Harry's main action is to find out whether he is good or evil.

- First, we are told that only the evil Heir of Slytherin can open the Chamber of Secrets.
- Next, Harry hears a strange voice no one else can hear, a voice that says "Kill!" When Harry tells Ron and Hermione about the voice, they warn him that, even for a wizard, hearing voices is a bad sign.
- Next, Harry speaks Parseltongue (snake language) to a snake. Ron and Hermione explain that Slytherin spoke Parseltongue, and it is believed that only evil wizards can talk to snakes.
- Evidence seems to be pointing towards Harry as the Heir of Slytherin, though Harry doesn't want that to be true.
- Next, Harry seeks information from the Sorting Hat, a device used to place incoming student wizards in one of four dormitories. Originally the Hat wanted to place him in Slytherin House (the dormitory for evil wizards), but Harry protested and was sent to Gryffindor instead. Now he asks the Hat if it put him in the right house. Harry is questioning who he is.
- Later, Harry defeats the Basilisk (BIG snake). Even after this victory, Harry worries about whether he is an evil wizard.
- Near the end of the film, Harry turns to Professor Dumbledore (*raisonneur*) for the answer to his question of identity. Dumbledore explains that Harry does have many of the same qualities as the evil Lord Voldemort but implies that Harry chooses to use his abilities to pursue different goals than Voldemort's: to pursue good rather than evil. Dumbledore speaks the following line of dialogue, putting Harry's adventures into a philosophical perspective:
"It's not the abilities we possess that show who we really are; it's the choices we make."

Dumbledore's response to Harry's question is a thematic statement. Scripts do not often provide thematic statements so overtly.

Looking, then, for a **thematic subject** and **thematic statement** consistent with the main action of the film and Dumbledore's philosophical statement, we could make a case for the following:

- **Thematic subject**: "the nature of human identity—what makes a person good or evil."
- **Thematic statement**: "In *Harry Potter and the Chamber of Secrets*, J.K. Rowling shows that it's not the abilities that human beings possess that show who we truly are: it's the choices we make."
- Please notice that adding the introductory format to a thematic subject *does not change* the subject into a thematic statement: "In *Harry Potter and the Chamber of Secrets*, J.K. Rowling explores the nature of human identity — what makes a person good or evil." What follows the introductory format is still a phrase, not a complete sentence. Adding the introductory format doesn't tell the reader what Rowling is showing us *about* the nature of human identity and/or what makes a person good or evil .

Consider the following questions when looking for philosophical statements by characters:

- Do any of the characters make statements about the meaning of some aspect of human existence?
- Do these statements provide you with insight into the main action of the story?
- Does the statement merely represent the individual character's idea about life, or does it seem to help explain the meaning of what happens in the story?

5. **Contradictions and structural oddities**
   When a script seems traditionally constructed up through the major crisis but later departs from usual structure, we may speculate that the playwright is deliberately contradicting audience expectations. Why? Probably the structural twist points the audience towards thematic ideas the author wants them to see. In order to analyze a script's meaning fully in such a case, we may need to go outside the script itself and do research about the playwright and the socio-historical context surrounding the writing of the script.

Tartuffe provides a clear example of a departure from traditional structure that poses challenges to anyone seeking to interpret the script's meaning. Up until the major crisis, Orgon clings to his view of Tartuffe as the embodiment of religious perfection. As he tells Cléante when his brother-in-law tries to suggest that Tartuffe may be a fraud:

Orgon	...'Twas heaven that made me bring him to my house;
	And since that time, everything prospers here.
	He censures everything, and for my honor
	He takes an active interest in my wife,
	Warns me when people look too kindly at her—
	He's twice as jealous of her as I could be.
	You can't imagine his religious scruples!
	The merest trifle is a sin to him;
	Nothing's too insignificant to shock him.
	Why, he accused himself the other day
	Of capturing a flea while he was praying,
	And pinching it to death with too much anger!

Cléante's attempt to force Orgon to see reason and get rid of Tartuffe (*trigger of the inciting incident*) causes Orgon to prove to his rebellious family who's boss in this household (*heap*). The first step Orgon takes is to announce he's going to marry Tartuffe to Marianne, Orgon's daughter. A series of major complications ensue in which each time Orgon's family members resist his domination, he retaliates — by giving more and more power to Tartuffe.

In the scene that triggers the major crisis, Elmire hides Orgon under a table so he can see for himself that Tartuffe is a lying lecher. Elmire invites Tartuffe to make another pass at her, but the wily hypocrite demands physical proof of her affection. Much of the comedy in the scene comes from the double meaning of Elmire's dialogue as she attempts to pry Orgon out from under the table by coughing to cue him to appear.

Tartuffe	... Content my longings, do not be afraid;
	All the responsibility is mine ...
	(*Elmire coughs*)

	You have a nasty cough.
Elmire	It tortures me.
Tartuffe	Perhaps you'd care to accept a licorice cough drop?
Elmire	It's a persistent cold, and I'm afraid
	That all the cough drops in the world won't
	help it.
Tartuffe	Very distressing.
Elmire	More than I can say.
Tartuffe	Well, anyway, I can dispel your scruples.
	You are assured that I will keep the secret.
	Evil does not exist until it's published;
	It's worldly scandal that creates the offense;
	And sin in silence is not sin at all.
Elmire	(*coughs*) In short, I see that I shall have to yield,
	Make up my mind to grant you everything.
	Otherwise, I suppose, I can't convince
	One who is asking irrefutable proof …

Beneath the table, Orgon is undergoing a paradigm shift, discovering that Tartuffe is not a holy man but a hypocrite who would betray his benefactor. When Elmire finally drags Orgon out from his hiding place, Orgon's lines not only reflect his paradigm shift but his attempt to save face by claiming he was never fooled at all:

Orgon	(*springing forth*) … Aha! You holy man, you
	wanted to fool me!
	How rapidly you yielded to temptation!
	Wedding my daughter and lusting for my wife!
	I've long suspected things were not aboveboard;
	I always thought that you would change your style.
	But now the proof is carried far enough.
	I'm satisfied, and this is all I need.

The heap of the major crisis, the choice Orgon makes, is to confront Tartuffe and attempt to banish him from the house. Orgon continues trying to prove he's boss; however, Tartuffe turns the tables on him. Earlier, Orgon deeded the house to Tartuffe when he disinherited his son Damis, so Tartuffe now has the power to banish Orgon. Tartuffe also has the incriminating letters Orgon asked him to keep safe, so the villain threatens to denounce Orgon to the king. Orgon has tried to use Tartuffe to enhance his own power, only to discover that he has given away his power to Tartuffe. Like Oedipus, Orgon has gone through a paradigm shift at the major crisis, and like Oedipus, Orgon has experienced a fall from power.

Following the major crisis, Cléante points out Orgon's imprudence in giving all his property and secrets into the hands of Tartuffe. Orgon angrily asserts that he has learned his lesson and henceforth will never trust a religious man. Cléante, whom many scholars consider the script's *raisonneur*, then makes a famous speech in which he warns Orgon against going to extremes.

Cléante   Now there you go again, getting excited!
              You can't be moderate in anything.
              You never seem to find the sensible course;
              From one excess you fall into the other.
              You see your error, and you recognize
              That you were taken in by pious fraud;
              But now, to correct yourself, what reason is there
              That you should fall into a greater error,
              And lump the character of all worthy men
              With the character of a perfidious rascal?
              Because a blackguard boldly takes you in,
              Impersonating an austere believer,
              You would conclude that everyone's like him,
              And that no true believer now exists?
              Let the freethinkers draw those false conclusions.
              Distinguish virtue from its outward seeming,
              Never give your esteem too hastily,
              Keep to the reasonable middle way.
              Try not to give your honor to impostors,
              But don't insult genuine piety.
              And if you must choose one extreme or the other,
              Let your fault be excessive leniency.

Other evidence in the script would support a choice of "moderation instead of going to extremes" as a significant thematic subject in *Tartuffe*. One might decide that the script follows in the pattern of the Harry Potter example we analyzed above, in which the raisonneur provides the thematic statement. However, the story does not end with Cléante's philosophizing; more complications follow.

All the characters Orgon has previously mistreated try unsuccessfully to help him, but further complications make things worse and worse. Mme. Pernelle clings to her view of Tartuffe as saintly, and Orgon finds the tables turned on him again as he tries to convince his mother of Tartuffe's villainy, and she refuses to believe him. A bailiff comes to evict Orgon and the family from their home. Finally, Tartuffe, having turned over Orgon's friend's political papers to the authorities, shows up to gloat as the king's Officer arrests Orgon for treason.

The ending, however, provides a startling reversal, as the Officer arrests Tartuffe instead, restores Orgon's property, and pardons Orgon for his political offense *(structural climax)*. In a long speech, the Officer declares that the omniscient king (Louis XIV) sees through all fakery and dispenses true justice:

Officer   …(*To Orgon*) You've had a nasty scare; but
                 calm yourself.
                 Our present King is enemy of fraud,
                 His eyes can penetrate his subjects' hearts;
                 The art of charlatans cannot delude him.
                 And his great spirit, wise in the ways of men,
                 Watches his kingdom with discerning eyes.
                 No one can take him easily by surprise,
                 And his firm reason yields to no excess,
                 To worthy men he gives immortal glory,
                 And yet his zeal for virtue is not blind.
                 His love for genuine faith does not eclipse
                 The horror one should feel for false devotion …

As we pointed out in Chapter 3, usually an action taken by the protagonist provides the structural climax, unifying the root action of the script. The structural climax of *Tartuffe* seems contrived, since not only does the protagonist not resolve the script's main action but nothing in the structure of the script prepared for the means used to resolve the action. A contrived ending of this type is called *deus ex machina*, "god from the machine." The term comes from ancient Greek tragedy, in which (particularly in the scripts of Euripides) a playwright had altered the traditional legend or myth and therefore had to bring in a god, lowered to the stage in a crane-like machine, to fix the ending so the story would turn out the way it was supposed to.

The thematic ideas of excess and moderation reoccur in the Officer's final speech. However, when a structural oddity such as *deus ex machina* occurs in a script, the analyst would be wise to engage in historical and biographical research, seeking a reason for the variation in structure, a reason which might also impact the script's meaning.

Historical context of *Tartuffe*

Tartuffe (1664-69), by social satirist Jean-Baptiste Poquelin (aka Molière), proved highly controversial when first performed. The Archbishop of Paris threatened to excommunicate anybody who attended the play or even read the script. A Catholic secret society known as the Company of the Holy Sacrament (*Compagnie du Saint-Sacrement*) had apparently taken on the mission of serving as France's "moral police." Some scholars argue that this group may have been the target of Molière's mockery. Evidence suggests that the society joined the anti-*Tartuffe* uproar, but since the society was secret, its actual political goals and machinations remain mere conjecture.

King Louis XIV, the "Sun King," was Molière's patron, but even he forbade performances until 1669. Scholars speculate that politics, specifically power struggles between Church and State, played a role in the censorship and that when Louis emerged victorious, he permitted Molière to stage *Tartuffe*. Since Molière revised the script at least twice in his attempts to reverse the ban, and the original version has not survived, we don't know how much that version actually attacked religion, as opposed to religious hypocrisy. Evidence in written attacks suggests that Tartuffe originally wore a priest's collar.

Given the context, one might assume that the ending of the final version served to thank, flatter, and/or support Molière's patron. Nonetheless, anyone producing *Tartuffe* today must decide how to handle the odd ending and whether it will (as structural climaxes usually do) affect the thematic interpretation of the script. Certainly, thematic subjects having to do with "excess vs. moderation" and "truth vs. illusion" can be found throughout the script as well as in the Officer's speech. However, the thematic subject of "power" can also be drawn from the action of the script. At the inciting incident, Orgon seeks to assert power over his family. At the major crisis, Orgon seeks to assert power over Tartuffe but instead loses power to Tartuffe. At the structural climax, Tartuffe seeks to exert power over Orgon and the king, but instead loses power to the king. Perhaps instead of *deus ex machina,* we should call the ending of *Tartuffe rex ex machina* — or "the king in the wings." In developing an interpretation of the play, an artistic team might consider issues of power, including "invisible" power exercised behind the scenes, as well as ideas about excess vs. moderation and truth vs. illusion.

While research into historical and biographical context may prove particularly useful in considering thematic implications of structural oddities, research may shed additional light on any script. You may disagree with other scholars' interpretations, but even an interpretation you disagree with can stimulate your own thinking.

What are the criteria for effective thematic statements?

1. The thematic statement must be in the correct format.
2. The thematic statement must be clearly stated.
3. The thematic statement must be justifiable on the basis of what happens in the script. The interpretation of life presented in the script may contradict your beliefs. You don't have to agree with the thematic statement; however, beware of imposing your own beliefs on a script if they don't fit what happens in the story.
4. Effective thematic statements grow out of a careful examination of all the meaning-bearing elements of the script. Don't ignore something essential to the story.
5. Effective thematic statements are specific to the script being analyzed. They focus attention on the script's unique and important elements.
6. Effective thematic statements say something significant about some aspect of human existence. What have I learned about life from this script?
7. Clichés are superficial and boring, thus aren't good thematic statements.
8. Effective thematic statements stimulate my creativity as an artist.

Capstone Assignment: Thematic Statements

Part A: Analysis

1. Write a thematic statement for the script for which you created an RAS. Compare the RAS with the complete thematic statement you just composed.
2. Do they fit together?
3. If not, revise either the RAS or the TS or both until the two match.
4. Once you're satisfied with your TS, write a thematic analysis for that script. Your TS will serve as the thesis for the essay.
5. Justify your thematic statement by explaining how it reflects your (possibly revised) RAS.
6. Give evidence from the script in terms of action, dialogue, patterns and/or imagery that supports your interpretation of the script's meaning.
7. Continue to revise your essay until you're satisfied with your TS, RAS, analysis, and support.

Part B: Mental Management: Reflection

Answer the first three questions plus a, b, **or** c in #4

1. Did the thematic analysis you just completed help you refine your RAS for the script?
2. In terms of your own thinking process, which task do you prefer to do first: TS or RAS?
3. Why?
4. Answer a, b, **or** c.
   a. What ideas from your own knowledge and experience did you use in developing your thematic analysis for the capstone exercise? Explain how you used these personal ideas.
   b. Did you gain any new insights into human life through reading and analyzing the script? If so, explain your new insights.
   c. Do you personally disagree with the understanding about human life you think the playwright communicates? If so, explain why you disagree.

Peer Review Checklists for Capstone Assignments can be found in Appendix B.

Chapter 8
The Central Production Metaphor

What is a central production metaphor?

As we've seen, a variety of components make up the structure of scripts. We've learned tools for analyzing those components, allowing us to extract specific types of information from the script. Now we're going to learn a tool that synthesizes all of our analytical work into one concise, overarching structure which will stimulate the imagination of production artists and audience members. This tool will help us articulate, in a succinct form, the interpretation our production will emphasize. We call this overarching structure a **central production metaphor**.

Sometimes, theatre artists will talk about the director's "concept" for a production. George Black in *Contemporary Stage Directing* uses the term "production matrix" for a *metaphor or model* that unifies all the production elements. We prefer the direct term "central production metaphor" for the concept that states the director's interpretation in the form of a metaphor.

How does a metaphor work?

Because we're going to be expressing the central interpretation of the production in the form of a metaphor, we should take a look at how metaphors in general work. First, metaphors have a specific form. In his essay in *Metaphor and Thought*, Allan Paivio suggests there are three parts to a metaphor: the **topic**, the **vehicle**, and the **ground**. The topic is the thing we want to know more about. The second term in the metaphor is called "the vehicle" because it transfers, or carries over, its qualities to the topic. The things the topic and vehicle have in common form the *ground*.

"My love is a red, red rose."

What are some of the qualities that my love and a rose might have in common?

Figure 8:1

The Structure of a Metaphor.

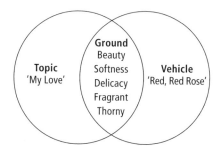

In the above example, "my love" is the *topic*. I'm comparing my love to "a red, red rose" (the *vehicle*) and implying that the two are similar. I know what a rose is, but I may not be sure what love is. In comparing the topic to the vehicle, I learn things about the topic that I might not have discovered without the metaphor. For instance, I might have realized that "my love" is beautiful but not thought about her fragrance. Maybe I recognized that love feels soft — but not that I need to look out for thorns (Ouch! Love can hurt). The list of qualities that form the ground help me understand the unknown (love) in terms of the known (a rose).

EXERCISE 8:1

Thinking about the ground

1. Add to the list of qualities shared by "my love" and a rose. How many can you find? Try to find some similarities that aren't at all obvious.
2. What images arise in your mind's eye as you picture the metaphor "My love is a red, red rose?"
3. Think about the thinking process you used to develop the "ground" list. As you were looking for similarities between the rose and "my love", you probably thought first of qualities you associate with a rose. Then you asked yourself if each quality also could apply to "my love." Why?

There is more than one type of metaphor.

A. Metaphoric thinking that humans use all the time is the kind of metaphor that *makes the strange familiar*. In other words, we use something that's known to communicate or speculate about something less well-known. For example, there used to be a gasoline ad that said, "Put a tiger in your tank!" This brand of gas may have been unknown to you, but the metaphor suggested that the brand would perform like something you do know: a tiger, fierce and powerful. Indeed, if you want to describe to me anything with which I'm not familiar, one way to do that is with a metaphor.

B. A different type of metaphor *makes the familiar strange*. In this type of thinking, the topic is known, and the vehicle is known, but we don't usually think of the two as related. The unexpected juxtaposition of vehicle and topic makes us look at the topic from a new perspective. For instance, Paivio suggests that a metaphor is an eclipse of the sun. Why do you think he uses that metaphor to explain the essence of what a metaphor is?

In chapter 1 of this book, we examined analogies; in chapter 5, we asked you to find a personal analogy to use in developing a character. What's the difference between analogies and metaphors? To be honest, that difference is so cloudy that some scholars use the terms interchangeably. Holyoak and Thagard argue that metaphor requires many of the same thinking processes as analogy, but that in metaphor the two domains, or fields, from which come the two items being compared are farther apart. Robert and Michèle Root-Bernstein emphasize the emotional power packed by the condensed image in a metaphor. Both analogy and metaphor require a mental "leap" to bring together two objects or concepts similar in some but not all ways — and for which the juxtaposition of the two gives new insight into at least one of them.

One possible way to think about the difference between analogies and metaphors is that analogies have four terms implicit, if not overtly stated. For instance, in chapter 1, we gave the example: toes: feet :: fingers: hands. In our metaphor above, however, there are only two terms: my love (topic) and "a red, red rose" (vehicle). We could use the domains, or categories, from which the topic and vehicle come as implicit terms: my love: all human emotions : a red, red rose: all flowers. However, this analogy doesn't seem to suggest quite the same meaning as the metaphor.

The way we use the terms in this book, a metaphor encourages us to brainstorm about the multiple ways in which the familiar and unfamiliar items are similar; we list these similarities as we think about the "ground." An analogy, on the other hand, wants us to focus our attention on a particular way the two items are similar, usually in terms of their function or relationship to another pair of items.

By the way, be careful not to mix up metaphors and similes. In a *simile*, I compare my love to a rose and *say* that the two are alike.

"My love is *like* a red, red rose."

A metaphor makes the same kind of comparison but leaves out the word "like." A metaphor is stronger, so we want to use that form in our work.

EXERCISE 8:2

Thinking about metaphors and analogies

1. Explore the following three metaphors, jotting down the list of shared qualities, the *ground.*
   • A school is a factory
   • A school is a business
   • A school is a garden
2. Now use each metaphor to develop an analogy:
   • If a school is a factory, a student is _____
   • If a school is a business, a student is _____
   • If a school is a garden, a student is _____
3. Since you are a student, what is implied about you if a school is a factory? If it is a business? A garden?
4. *Reflection and discussion:*
   • Which of the "school" metaphors most accurately captures your experience of school?
   • Which of the "school" metaphors captures what you want school to be?
   • What are other metaphors for school?
   • What have you learned from this exercise?

When we create a central production metaphor, the script itself is the *topic.* The thing to which we compare the script is the *vehicle.* For example: *Arms and the Man (topic)* is a fractured fairytale (*vehicle*). The ground, the elements or qualities that the two share, is emphasized by the metaphor. So we now know what *form* the interpretation (or concept) takes: it's a metaphor in which the script is the topic.

Why use a central production metaphor?

Why is the metaphor form *useful* to theatrical artists? There are three main reasons:

1. The metaphor unifies the production. The director communicates the central production metaphor to the designers, and the team creates all production elements based on that image. They come together to explore common "ground."
2. Metaphors stimulate the creative imagination. A central production metaphor is usually of the type that *makes the familiar strange*. In other words, it helps the creative team look at the script from a new perspective, often inspiring ideas for the actors as well as the designers and director.
3. The metaphor relates to the thematic statement. As a result, the artistic team's creative ideas help the audience understand the director's view of the play's meaning.

Who creates the central production metaphor?

The Central Production Metaphor can be created in several ways or some combination thereof.

1. The director may have formed a strong interpretation based on her analysis and may bring his/her metaphor to the early production meetings. She may then ask the team of artistic collaborators to work with the metaphor in their designs.
2. The second method starts with one or more designers with strong interpretations who present their ideas to the director early in the production process. The director may agree to the proposed metaphor.
3. Third, the artistic collaborators brainstorm about ideas for a metaphor stimulated by their collective analysis. During several meetings, a metaphor emerges from the team.

Whatever method is used, it is the director who ultimately determines what metaphor best reflects her thematic statement. Regardless of who created the metaphor, all artistic team members use it as the basis of their creative work.

How do I find a central production metaphor?

The search for a metaphor is not a logical process; it is *a creative* process. Humans haven't yet figured out exactly how creativity works. We have, however, realized that creativity doesn't arise in a vacuum — the fires of imagination must be fed. A lot of hard work and thought go into giving the creative self the nourishment it needs in order to come up with creative ideas.

Maybe the best way to explain the process of generating a central production metaphor is with a metaphor: *The production process is a garden.* What does our topic, the production process, have in common with our vehicle, a garden?

- *Till the ground.* Analyze the script, using all the tools you've learned so far. Pay particular attention to images and patterns in the script itself. Interpret the story — what meanings strike you, emotionally as well as intellectually?
- *Plant your "seed" early and tend to it often.* As with the seeds in our metaphorical garden, lots of time is needed for nature to do its work of germination, growth, and maturation. Read the script early and often.
- *Nourish the soil.*
  a. Do research on the script and its historical context.
  b. Study other scripts by the same author.
  c. Read what scholars have to say about the script.
  d. Listen to music of the time period.
  e. Look at the art of the time period.
  f. Browse through your own personal library of art, music, poetry — your favorite things. What stimulates you artistically and intellectually?
  g. Does the script suggest to you the work of a particular artist or musician?
  h. Does it remind you of a significant experience in your life?
  i. Imagine yourself falling into the world of the story, as Alice fell down the rabbit hole. Wander through this world in your imagination. What strikes you? Images, sounds, smells, feelings?
- *Give the garden time to grow.* After you've nourished your creative self, let nature take its course. Do something else for

a while. The metaphor may come to you while you're in the shower or driving down the street thinking about what you're going to give your mother for her birthday.

- *Keep an eye out for green shoots.* Look! A little green growing thing is poking up through the ground. Is it a seedling production metaphor … or crab grass?
- *Weed your garden.* You want to test each metaphor that arises. Not every one may be a "keeper." Use critical thinking to separate the weeds from the sprouts. Evaluate each metaphor according to the list of criteria below.
- *Harvest the fruit of your labors.* When the harvest comes in, if the metaphor is a good one, you will feel elated. Your intuition will cry "Aha!" Delicious ideas for carrying it out in production will start to drop into your lap. The creative self is ready to play! Have fun!

What are the criteria for a central production metaphor?

Practice critical thinking again. Use the following criteria to evaluate your production metaphor:

1. The image you choose must be a metaphor for the script itself. Example: "*Arms and the Man* is a fractured fairytale."
2. The metaphor must correspond with and help to communicate the thematic statement you've chosen as your interpretation of the script.
3. The metaphor must help to unify the production.
4. The metaphor should provide new insight into the story.
5. The metaphor should stimulate your creativity. It should help communicate your interpretation of the script to your artistic collaborators, inspiring design, directing, and acting choices that assist the audience in experiencing your interpretation of the story's meaning.
6. Review the list below of types of metaphors that are *not* useful. Make sure that your choice of metaphor is not *just a historical period, done for novelty's sake, bizarre, a classification of what the script is, or a metaphor for a character rather than*

the script itself. The following types do not work as a central production metaphor.

- A concept that just sets a script in a historical time period, for example: "We'll do *Oedipus* in the 1960s." Or "We'll set *Hamlet* in Nazi Germany." A director who decides arbitrarily on a historical period without articulating what meaning that choice communicates gives the "concept" production a bad name. And to say, "we'll do a modern updating of _____ [any script]" is NOT a central production metaphor. Ask yourself *why* you want to set *Hamlet* in Nazi Germany. What thematic interpretation would such a choice communicate? What's the metaphor?
- A metaphor that has no relationship to the meaning of the script but is done for novelty's sake, for example: "We'll do *Oedipus* as a tic-tac-toe game!"
- A metaphor that draws together things with superficially related meanings but for which the execution would be so bizarre that tragedy would become farce. For instance, one student team decided that *Oedipus* is the film *Titanic* because both have to do with pride going before a fall ("they said she'd never go down"). The most appalling design element the group presented had Oedipus wearing a crown in the shape of a ship.
- A metaphor that isn't really a metaphor but a classification or description of what the script *is*, for example, "We'll do *Hamlet* as a tragedy." Remember that you're looking for the type of metaphor that makes the familiar strange and inspires creativity because it provides a new perspective.
- A metaphor in which the topic isn't the script as a whole but a character in the script, for example, "We'll do *Tartuffe* as a sneaky weasel."

Let's work through the process of creating a Central Production Metaphor together with the following two examples. First we will look at the Central Production Metaphor that guided a production of *Tartuffe*.

Example 8:1 *Tartuffe*

In winter 2000, this vision of *Tartuffe* was staged. The interpretation reflects *the year in which the play was performed*, the change of millennium. Another influence: a famous production of *Tartuffe* directed by Roger Planchon in Paris in 1972, which explored 17th century political power issues in a time of transition from the power of the family to the power of the Church to the power of the centralized state (King Louis XIV).

> **Thematic Statement:** In *Tartuffe*, Moliere reveals that individual control over events is an illusion; and our contemporary world is a "show," a crazy, distorted circus run by an invisible (possibly corporate) power.

> **Central Production Metaphor:** *Tartuffe* is an apocalyptic millennium circus, in the manner of Ray Bradbury's *Something Wicked This Way Comes*.

NOTES from director's analysis:
The turn of the millennium is a time of shifting power (perhaps from the industrial to the information age; from the nation-state to the global corporation). Fear, verging on panic, reigns. The middle class seeks refuge in religion. An alliance between religion and government (King Louis XIV, representing the nation-state) tries to maintain control. However, this alliance is uneasy and suspicious on both sides.

Orgon, panicking, has plunged headlong into religion. He has regressed into a childlike state (the "circus"). Orgon is the patriarch, ringmaster of the circus — it is his "show" — but his family plots rebellion. They grasp onto Tartuffe as a scapegoat — if they can evict Tartuffe, they can regain the "normal state of affairs," their endangered security.

Tartuffe appears as a "clown," a "hypocrite," a threat to the family, salvation to Orgon. He does not yet appear in his true demonic and dangerous form. He has a secret alliance with the government, which will ultimately betray him.

It's a media circus, a millenium "show," a world of smoke and mirrors; nothing is what it seems. A huge and ominous silhouette of a laughing clown appears on the screen upstage at key moments. The silhouette bobs robotically up and down as it laughs: loud, electronically distorted laughter. In the amusement park in my home town, such a clown sat at the entrance to the maze of mirrors. When I was a child, its laughter and mechanical movement always made me shiver. In this production, the silhouette turns out to be Louis XIV, in "evil" clown costume. It's as if he's been the hidden audience and power behind the scenes for this "performance."

Time is cyclical or spiral. The pace of life is fast and getting faster: the carousel image from *Something Wicked*. As time spins out of control, characters may regress to childhood.

The play starts very slapstick, very physical humor. It becomes darker and darker. There are moments when the lights go down and the nasty laughing clown silhouette appears on the scrim. This play is a dark farce, both comic and dangerous.

Figure 8:2
Orgon

Who is really the puppet-master here? First banner: "Orgon's apocalyptic millenium circus." Orgon thinks he runs the show. Then when Tartuffe gets control, second banner — "Tartuffe's apocalyptic millenium circus." third banner (when Louis XIV double-crosses Tartuffe): "Louis's apocalyptic millenium circus." Then at the end of the show, the banner changes to: "www//???.org's apocalyptic millenium circus." When the last banner appears, all the characters transform into robotic puppets. The play investigates layers and layers of power and illusion.

Costume design for Orgon by James M. Miller, Professor of Theatre, University of Missouri. Production of *Tartuffe*, directed by Suzanne Burgoyne, University of Missouri, February 2000.

Each character is a circus character:

Orgon, the Ringmaster

Tartuffe, hobo-type sad clown (Emmett Kelly)

Dorine, the gypsy fortune teller

Valère, the daring young man on the flying trapeze

Mme Pernelle, the fat lady (fat suit)

Cléante, the tightrope walker

Damis, the circus strong man

Mariane, the kewpie doll
Elmire, the bareback rider
Loyal, the lion tamer
King's Officer, carnival barker
Flipote, Madame Pernelle's maid (played by a large man), and Tartuffe's serving man Laurent (played by a small woman) are roustabout clowns. They're really Louis XIV's spies in disguise. They pull off their wigs and pull out their guns in the last scene. First they point their guns at Orgon, then swing to point them at Tartuffe when the Officer names him as the culprit.

Figure 8:3
Tartuffe

Costume design for Tartuffe by James M. Miller, Professor of Theatre, University of Missouri.

The stage set: abstract? ramps & platforms? trampoline? circus ring? tent? house of mirrors? Chase lights!!!! Everything is **distorted**, seen in a funhouse mirror. Can we do the trapeze bit with Valère? If so, probably need a platform for Valère to climb and swing. Do we still have the carousel horses? Can they be ridden? Can we do a turning carousel?

Figure 8:4
Elmire

Costume design for Elmire by James M. Miller, Professor of Theatre, University of Missouri.

Production photograph
of *Tartuffe*, directed
by Suzanne Burgoyne,
University of Missouri,
February 2000. Scenic
design by R. Dean
Packard.

Figure 8:5

Tartuffe
production

The "closet" might be a distorted door in the set — or
a magician's trunk set up on
end (possibly with knives
piercing it).

The table under which Orgon
hides might be Dorine's fortune-telling table, with a
crystal ball attached to the
top. The crystal ball is actually an upside-down fishbowl,
so Orgon can poke his head up through it at times during the
scene in which Tartuffe attempts to seduce Elmire.

Props: Each character has a prop befitting the circus character
which can be used for character business. For instance, Damis
— the circus strongman — carries a (fake) barbell. He can threat-
en other characters with it.
Orgon-as-ringmaster car-
ries a whip. Cléante, the
tightrope walker, carries a
pole and uses it to balance
himself. Madame Pernelle,
the "fat lady," carries a slapstick which she uses to beat
Flipote.

Costumes are circus cos-
tumes appropriate for the
circus role each character
plays. Bright and clown-
ish — lots of color! Clown
make-up.

Tartuffe grabs Orgon's top
hat and whip when Orgon
denounces him and Tartuffe
takes overt control of the
house.

Figure 8:6

Tartuffe
production

Madame Pernelle beating Flipote with the slapstick, *Tartuffe*, University of Missouri, February
2000.

Calliope music, the kind that plays for a carousel. The music becomes distorted, speeds up and slows down.

If possible, the circus performers "set up" at least some aspects of the set when they arrive onstage. There should be a "parade" of the performers to begin the show. Possibly the performance atmosphere should start in the

The table scene, *Tartuffe*, University of Missouri, February, 2000.

lobby, with fortune-telling booth, juggling acts, etc. "Welcome" the audience into the show. After all, they're part of the "show," puppets of the hidden powers that manipulate human life.

Figure 8:7
Tartuffe
production

Tartuffe seducing Elmire, *Tartuffe*, University of Missouri, February, 2000.

Example 8:2 *Avatar*

Our second example is *Avatar*. The film has already been made, and we don't have the opportunity to ask the artistic team if they worked with a central production metaphor. However, we can read what an experienced script analyst thinks the central metaphor might be and how she supports her interpretation with evidence from the film.

Thematic Statement: *Avatar* draft #7: "In *Avatar,* James Cameron shows that 'civilized' humans have lost our spiritual connections and become greedy materialistic monsters, but if we can walk a mile in the moccasins of a 'whole'

Figure 8:8
Tartuffe
production

being and learn to see the natural world through uncluttered eyes, we can shed our corrupted egos and transform into spiritual beings, restoring our connections with all life and the cosmic whole."

Central Production Metaphor: *Avatar* is a return to lost Paradise. Powerful central images in the film are both trees: Home Tree and the Tree of Souls. Home Tree bears with it all the connotations of Home and Homecoming. The Tree of Souls is divine, allowing connection with the deity and all life. In Christianity, a tree is the traditional symbol of the Garden of Eden. The tree image and its implications struck me forcefully the very first time I saw the film.

My interpretation of the meaning of the story deals with the idea of "fallen" humanity that has lost its spiritual connection but can regain it. The metaphor I see Cameron using in his film corresponds with the thematic statement I derived from my viewing of the film.

Visual choices in the film carry out aspects of the central metaphor. We discussed in the given circumstances chapter the contrast between the "fallen" mechanized world of the earthmen and the Edenic natural world of the Na'vi. This difference is heightened by the radiant iridescence of the forest vs. the dull metallic sheen of the indoor corporate headquarters. The natural world is glowingly alive and beautiful, while the corporate world is dreary and claustrophobic. The living creatures in the Na'vi world appear healthy, graceful, and energetic. The earthmen's complexions, by comparison, are dull. Jake looks pale in his human form, to say nothing of his withered legs. The mechanized monster attack robots worn by the Colonel and others symbolize how "fallen" humans have transformed into machines.

The whole natural world of Pandora is connected by a network of divine energy that becomes visible during the ritual scenes, as the Na'vi move across the ground, and as Jake touches flowers. The Na'vi and some of the animals have appendages which allow them to "bond" with each other energetically/psychically.

Aural aspects of the film also reflect the metaphor. The soundtrack for the forest scenes is hauntingly alluring when it's not heart-wrenching. The obnoxious noise of machinery and weapons adds to the sense that the corporate headquarters is a world from which a sensitive being wants to escape.

The first image we see in the film is the landscape of Pandora, and we hear Jake's voice-over telling us that we are seeing the dream of flying that has haunted him ever since he lost the use of his legs in battle. Pandora is thus immediately associated with Jake's sense of loss, an image embedded deep in his psyche that guides him home.

Finally, as supporting evidence for my interpretation, I'll point out that the lyrics of the theme song (which I didn't actually decipher until after I identified the central metaphor) include a line about love showing the singer the pathway to "Paradise."

<table>
<tr><td>

1. By yourself or in a group, imagine you are going to direct and design a production of a dramatic adaptation of the following nursery rhyme.

> Little Miss Muffet
> Sat on a tuffet
> Eating her curds and whey.
> Along came a spider
> And sat down beside her
> And frightened Miss Muffet away.

2. Choose a central production metaphor.
3. Justify your choice with a **thematic analysis** of the "script," and explain how your central production metaphor will affect the following:

- Scenic design
- Sound design
- Costume design
- Lighting design
- Props
- Make-up
- Acting choices
- Movement patterns

Sample Metaphors

- "Miss Muffet" is *A Midsummer Night's Dream*, but the dream turns into a nightmare.
- "Miss Muffet" is an apocalyptic vision.
- "Miss Muffet" is a Creation Myth.
- "Miss Muffet" is a Native American ritual featuring the archetypal spider trickster figure.
- "Miss Muffet" is a low-grade sci-fi movie.
- "Miss Muffet" is a Disney cartoon.

</td><td>

EXERCISE 8:3

Making a metaphor for Miss Muffet

</td></tr>
</table>

Capstone Assignment: Central Production Metaphor

Part A: "Triple Threat" Thinking

This project gives you an opportunity to use all the tools of script analysis you have learned in this text. It also asks you to think like a designer.

1. With a small group of classmates, choose an assigned script you have read this semester.
2. Imagine you are the production team for this script. Within your group, each of you choose a different element to design: scenery, costumes, lighting, make-up, props, or sound.
3. You have an unlimited budget and the theatre of your choice! No need to consider cost in your analysis.
4. Study the script carefully to discover all its given circumstances and how they will affect the play you're going to design.
5. Analyze the script for structure, character, and theme.
6. Together, decide on a central production metaphor.
7. Justify your choice of metaphor, including the relationship between the metaphor and the thematic statement.
8. Prepare for the next production meeting by writing an essay in which you explain and justify your central production metaphor, supporting it with a brief analysis of the script and your thematic statement. Explain how your design for your chosen area will implement the production metaphor, and describe how each design element you choose relates to the metaphor
9. Prepare visual (or aural, in case of sound design) aids that will help your team understand your design ideas. You do not actually have to design the production, unless you want to. Focus on aids that help the viewer understand your idea in terms of line, color, shape, use of space, historical period, sound quality, etc.
10. If you are the Sound Designer bring sound samples.
11. Meet again with your production team and present your design ideas.

Part B: Mental Management: Reflectiion
1. Which of the suggestions for finding a central production metaphor did you find most helpful?
2. Explain in as much detail as you can the thinking process that led to your choice of metaphor.
3. Identify two production metaphors you considered before settling on your final choice. Using the criteria for central metaphors, explain why you believe your choice was better than the other two.

Peer Review Checklists for Capstone Assignments can be found in Appendix B.

Appendices

What will I find in the Appendices?

The Appendices consist of two parts: Appendix A contains additional exercises, examples, assignments, models of completed assignments and materials for some chapters. Appendix B contains Peer Review Checklists to accompany each Capstone Assignment. The Appendices are arranged by chapter number and title.

Appendix A

Chapter 3: Action and Structure

Exercises Using Kinesthetic (Body) Thinking

Another kind of thinking is kinesthetic — thinking with our bodies. Athletes and dancers do this kind of thinking. The basketball player must learn not only how to throw the ball but how the ball *feels* in his hands, how his feet feel on the floor, how his whole body feels as he leaps to throw the ball into the basket. Dancers need to feel how their bodies shape space as they move through it. Other types of artists, and even scientists, use the physical and emotional sensations arising in their bodies as ways of solving problems and making discoveries.

1. **Conflict**
   Arm wrestle with a friend or classmate. If you're fairly evenly matched, the advantage moves back and forth between you. Each time that happens the suspense heightens. Actually, arm-wrestling while playing a scene is a good acting exercise. Physicalizing the conflict and discovering when the lead

shifts from one character to the other gives actors a sense of the dramatic structure of the scene.

2. **Major Crisis**

   Remember the Cyclops from *The Odyssey*? The one-eyed monster who holds Odysseus and his men captive in the cave? All members of the class will pretend to be Cyclops simultaneously. Think of yourself as an actor playing this creature from Greek mythology. Musical accompaniment, such as a strident and a peaceful track from Vangelis' "Heaven and Hell," would add to the experience.

   In order to play "Cyclops," put your hands together so they form a circular tunnel, thumbs at the bottom of the circle. Hold your hands in front of your eyes so you can only see through the tunnel they form.

   Everyone moves through the open space during the strident music. Since Cyclops is a selfish, grumpy guy, he bumps into others as he pushes through the crowd. He won't apologize either! He mutters and growls every time he bumps into someone.

   When the music stops, everyone stops. Close your eyes. Don't talk. Wait for the music to start, now the peaceful track. When it does, move through space again. You are now like Cyclops after Odysseus put out its one huge eye: blind. Suddenly, your whole relationship to the world has changed. Feel your way carefully into this new world, trying your utmost not to bump into anyone or anything. Don't talk. Listen to the music.

   Discussion Points
   a. What was it like to be the Cyclops with its one eye?
   b. What sensations did you feel in your body?
   c. What emotions did you experience by moving in this way?
   d. Is there anything in that experience that reminds you of today's world?
   e. What did it feel like suddenly to be blind?
   f. How did your relationship to the world change?

g. In what ways might this exercise relate to Oedipus?

h. Did you gain any insight into *Oedipus the King* through this experiment with kinesthetic thinking?

Chapter 4: Root Action Statement

Exercise Using Kinesthetic Thinking: Abstraction

Everyone in the class walks around in an empty space. There should be no talking throughout this exercise. When requested to do so, group yourselves according to the following classifying elements:

1. Shoe color
2. Hair color
3. Eye color
4. Skin color
5. Political affiliation

Discussion Points

a. Did you have any difficulty in abstracting and thus forming groups?

b. If so, why?

c. What emotions did you feel during the exercise?

d. Why?

Model: Structural Analysis Essay for *Oedipus the King*

In *Oedipus the King*, Sophocles employs the basic pattern of the detective story to explore the relationship between humankind and fate. As the play progresses, Oedipus's search for the murderer who has polluted the city transforms into a quest for his own identity. Proud of his intellectual prowess, Oedipus believes he knows who he is, and he thinks himself clever enough to escape the destiny predicted for him. The play proves him wrong. My root action statement for *Oedipus*: this script is about a willful, spiritually blind man who seeks to wrest the truth from life with his intelligence, but when he discovers life is ruled by fate, he trades physical sight for spiritual insight and surrenders to the will of the gods.

Sophocles presents a beginning stasis in which a plague has been devastating Thebes. A chorus of citizens is on their way to plead with King Oedipus, who once saved the city by answering the Sphinx's riddle, to save the city again — this time, from the plague. Before the play began, Oedipus sent his brother-in-law Creon to consult the oracle about the cause of the disease.

Creon returns with the oracle's message that the plague has occurred to punish the city for harboring the murderer of Laius, the previous king. Creon's announcement provides the inciting incident, triggering the main action: Trusting in his own intelligence to discern the truth, Oedipus himself sets off on a quest to find the murderer of Laius. Oedipus's quest prompts the major dramatic question: Will Oedipus find the murderer?

As the action proceeds, however, the major dramatic question evolves with each major complication, reaching new levels of significance. As the detective trying to solve the murder, Oedipus first sends for the blind prophet, Tiresias, to interrogate him. Tiresias, however, refuses to help, and he and Oedipus quarrel. When Oedipus misinterprets Tiresias' reluctance to answer questions as implying that the prophet is guilty of the crime, the seer accuses Oedipus himself of the murder. Tiresias' accusation provides the first major complication. As the result of Tiresias' accusation, Oedipus blindly jumps to the conclusion that Tiresias and Creon are plotting to overthrow him and threatens the traitors. At this point, the major dramatic question changes: Is Oedipus indeed the killer he seeks? Who "sees" things more clearly, the sighted but hot-tempered king or the blind prophet?

A second major complication occurs when Oedipus' wife Jocasta, attempting to smooth over the quarrel, warns Oedipus not to trust prophets. She gives an example: the oracle had told Laius he would be killed by his own son, but instead the baby was put out on a mountain to die; and Laius was murdered by robbers at a place where three roads meet. Jocasta's revelation, the second complication, starts Oedipus worrying; he suddenly remembers that he once killed an old man at a place where three roads meet. As a result, Oedipus sends for the only survivor of the attack, a shepherd who had reported that multiple robbers, not a single assassin, killed Laius. Again trusting his own intelligence, Oedipus reasons that if the shepherd sticks to his story, Oedipus himself cannot be guilty. The major dramatic question has again evolved:

Can oracles be trusted? Will Oedipus prove to be the murderer even though his guilt would contradict the oracle?

In the meantime, a messenger from Corinth arrives and informs Oedipus that his father, King Polybus, has died. Oedipus refuses to return to Corinth, however, citing an oracle warning him he was destined to kill his father and marry his mother. Since his mother still lives, he won't risk fulfilling that horrid fate. "No problem," the messenger replies. "She's not really your mother. You were adopted." The messenger reveals that he himself had been given the baby Oedipus by a Theban shepherd. The revelation that Oedipus is not who he thought he was is the third major complication. In spite of warnings from Jocasta that he shouldn't try to find out his real identity, Oedipus persists in his search for truth: he sends for the shepherd. With this complication, the major dramatic question shifts to: Who is Oedipus? The simple detective story has become a search for the nature of human identity.

The shepherd arrives (by one of those quirks of fate common in Greek tragedy, the shepherd who witnessed Laius' murder is the same one who gave the messenger the baby). Under interrogation, the shepherd finally admits that Oedipus is the son of Laius and Jocasta, his father's murderer and his mother's husband — Oedipus has unwittingly fulfilled the prophesy. This revelation is the fourth complication, which triggers the major crisis: Oedipus undergoes a change of world view, a paradigm shift. What choice will Oedipus make? What will Oedipus do now that he knows destiny does rule human life? The major dramatic question shifts to one related to the meaning of the play: What should be the response of an ethical human being to unbearable self-discovery?

Although Jocasta kills herself, Oedipus does not. He blinds himself, but he remains alive, believing his life has some yet-to-be-disclosed divine purpose. The choice to blind himself is the "heap" of the complication that triggered the major crisis. If the audience could actually see Oedipus blind himself, the blinding might provide the major emotional climax. However, the conventions of Greek tragedy precluded showing violence onstage — and there are three more scenes until the play ends.

Physically blind, Oedipus now possesses spiritual insight. He does not indulge in whining and blaming the gods for his downfall but instead takes responsibility for his own actions. When the chorus asks him, "Who has done this to you?" he replies, "Apollo. ... But the blinding hands are my own."

Still, however, Oedipus tries to assert his will. He demands, first of the Chorus and then of Creon, that he be sent into exile. In the fifth complication, Creon refuses because the new king believes he must consult the oracle to discover the god's will in the matter. Creon reminds Oedipus that he has lost the power he once had as king and now must obey.

Oedipus does not respond verbally to Creon's challenge. The stage directions indicate that everyone exits into the house except the Chorus. Yet Oedipus's choice not to argue but to submit to the will of the gods is the structural climax in my interpretation of the play. The actor playing Oedipus will need to make an acting choice that signifies his acceptance of divine will in a single moment that serves as the resolution of his main action. In order to emphasize the significance of the moment (and to avoid three anti-climactic scenes at the end of the play), Oedipus's choice or his walk to the house must be staged as the emotional climax.

It will take strong theatre artists — director, actor, and designers — to transform a mute moment (with no clues in the text) into the play's climax. One might imagine an Oedipus who sheds his willfulness and puts himself into the hands of the gods to lead where they will. One might imagine lights so blinding, terrible yet beautiful, that Oedipus becomes a silhouette feeling his way into a mysterious cosmos. Perhaps the scenery flies up into the sky so that Oedipus is walking into the sun. And sound ... ?

In the ending stasis of the play, Oedipus has gone off to follow where the gods will lead. The major dramatic questions have all been answered, for we now know who the murderer is, who Oedipus is — and we know the oracles spoke truth. Oedipus's response to his paradigm shift makes him a role model for the audience, as he feels his way into the spiritual realm hidden beneath the appearances of the material world — and the chorus warns us that Oedipus's self-discovery could be our own.

Chapter 5: Tools for Character Development

The examples, exercises, and models of character analysis below relate to *spines.*

Examples:

    A. *Arms and the Man*

        In *Arms and the Man*, Shaw attacks romantic ideals about love and war. In general, the characters can be divided between those who try to maintain the masks of false social ideals and those who try to rip the masks off.

        Root Action Statement: *Arms and the Man* is a play about a childlike man who unmasks romantic illusions in order to escape and punish his vulnerable romantic self, but when cornered by love confesses his need for nurturing and thus wins his mate.

        Character Spine for Bluntschli (protagonist): *To unmask romantic illusion* (strategy spine) *in order to control his own romantic folly* (goal spine). Bluntschli is "Mr. Practical." He sees the world as it is and calmly undercuts the romantic illusions of others. However, he can't admit to his own romantic feelings, which he masks until the major crisis. In Shaw's terminology, Bluntschli is a realist who is revealed as an idealist.

        I need to develop Bluntschli's biography to understand why he masks himself. The spine trigger seems connected to his relationship with his father — and he's notified of his father's death in the script. Clues in the script: Bluntschli ran away from home twice as a boy; he went into the army instead of his father's business. I envision Bluntschli's father as the living image of "practicality," who often berated his son for being an unmanly romantic. I imagine a scene in which nine-year-old Bluntschli spent all the money he'd saved on a box of chocolate creams for a girl he admired from afar. The girl laughed at him, and so did Dad. Perhaps young Bluntschli cried when rejected, and his father humiliated the child for being "womanish," and a fool for wasting his money. I suspect Bluntschli's "practicality" is the voice of the father he hears in his head.

Bluntschli must have been an idealist about war at some point. He went into the army — where he became disillusioned. So he's a realist because he's a disillusioned idealist. Does he feel secret disgust at himself for acting like Dad? For accepting his inheritance and using it to appease Raina's parents so he can win her? Bluntschli has inner conflict, but he masks it better than other characters. He's further down the road than they are, and his lessons have been bitter.

B. *Tartuffe*

Root Action Statement: This script is about a panic-stricken middle-class man who clings to a "divine" figure to protect his domination of his world, only to discover that his world has always been a puppet show, and he's never had any power at all.

Note: *Tartuffe* has an unusual structure; the protagonist does not take action as a result of his discovery, so there is no "result."

Character Spine for Orgon (protagonist): *to cling to control* (strategy spine) *in order to suppress his terror* (goal spine).

Civilization is in a state of transition, changing at a frantic pace. Orgon feels the earth turning to quicksand beneath his feet. Terrified by facing an unknown future, he regresses to childhood and seeks an all-powerful father-figure to protect him. He clings to "God" as embodied in Tartuffe — the one who can ensure his salvation, ensure he won't die, won't fall into the apocalyptic void of the future. His patriarchal power is threatened by feminism and the rebellion of the young. He fiercely clings to control of his family, which he also feels slipping away. He must dominate others in order to feel secure within himself.

Orgon's spine trigger: He was only a boy when a priest warned him that even to think of sex except for the purpose of procreation was a mortal sin that would send him straight to hell. A devout child, Orgon also had strong sexual urges. He feared the wrath of his domineering mother if she should ever "catch him in the act," and one day, to his horror and shame, she did. Since then, Orgon has developed into an authoritarian, dominating others to suppress his fear that he cannot control himself.

In reaction against his domineering mother, Orgon vowed that no woman would ever have power over him. He ruled his household with an iron hand. His first wife was meek and obedient — and not particularly attractive. With Elmire, a strong woman with sex appeal, Orgon often finds himself impotent. Thus the presence of Elmire shames him; she's a reminder of his failure. With its emphasis on chastity, religion will save him — enable Orgon to justify his lack of sexual prowess as purity. Therefore Tartuffe trying to seduce Elmire is an overwhelming betrayal that devastates Orgon

Exercise: Creating Character Metaphors

There are many kinds of thinking through which ideas may be explored deeply. So far, you have been using a lot of analytical and critical thinking to deconstruct the text and examine all the clues you could find about your character. Now you should do some imaginative thinking about your character and think more holistically and abstractly. You are going to create character metaphors for your character using abstract thinking, information already amassed from your text analysis, and a dash of creativity.

Write an essay in which you explore the answers to these questions. Be detailed and precise. Go beyond the superficial answer, being able to support your choices based on previous character analysis, what you have learned by "living in" your character's skin, and your intuition.

- Choose a texture that represents the essence of your character and discuss why you feel this to be true.
- Choose a sound that represents the essence of your character and discuss why you feel this to be true.
- Choose a shape that represents the essence of your character and discuss why you feel this to be true.
- Choose a food that represents the essence of your character and discuss why you feel this to be true.
- Choose an animal/plant that represents the essence of your character and discuss why you feel this to be true.

- Choose a color that represents the essence of your character and discuss why you feel this to be true.
- Choose a dynamic image that represents the essence of your character and discuss why you feel this to be true.

Model: Student-Authored Paper Creating Character Metaphors

When given this assignment and instructed to think more holistically, abstractly, and imaginatively, I found this task to be easier and more enjoyable than previous assignments. It was enjoyable for several different reasons, but most importantly, because I felt like I was prepared and confident in my knowledge to the point where I could rise to this challenge comfortably. I felt educated enough about the show, *A Chorus Line*, and about the character of Valerie Clark in particular, to make intellectual guesses about the questions I was asked to think about. With this belief in all of my past research and work, I was able to unleash my imaginative self and be confident that my answers were based on previous, supported material. I was able to connect and think about Valerie Clark in a different way, by undergoing the process of choosing a texture, sound, shape, food, animal, color, and dynamic image that best represent who/what the character of Val actually is.

When looking in a thesaurus, I found some synonyms of wicker: complexity, involvement, network, and snarl, to name a few. These synonyms that describe the texture of wicker can also be used to define Valerie Clark. She is complex in the way that there are two sides to Val. There is the sexy, sweet, performer side of Val, and then there's the earthy, sarcastic side to her that comes out during her monologue when her character is shown in more depth. At that moment, we know that there is more to her than just a pretty outward appearance. This similarity is analogous to a wicker chair due to the fact that its looks are deceiving. Upon first glance, a wicker chair does not look comfortable. However, once you sit in it, you are pleasantly surprised and become more inclined to it. This is true for the character of Valerie Clark. Based on her outward appearance, you would never be able to guess that she has a sailor's mouth, or that she has a plastic surgery secret, but once you learn those things, you tend to like the character of Val more, because she is not just another dumb, pretty girl with only her looks going for her.

Wicker is also a very pretty and intricate texture to look at and observe and while we know that Valerie is a very pretty woman, she is also a very interesting character. For example, when Zach asks what they are going to do when they can't dance anymore, Val responds, "Who cares? I don't care if I never dance another step as long as I live." At this point in the audition process, she is very honest and ballsy to say this to a director considering she is auditioning for a dancing chorus part. Furthermore, Val uses a lot of snarl words, such as "Fuck" and "Bitch," to shock and intrigue people, especially Zach. It is not a façade, however; that is just Val's personality. Another quality of Val's is her intelligence. One example of Val's intelligence is the fact that she is very observant and involved in the audition/moment at all times. Val really wants the job, not only to have an income, but also to work with Zach, add this show to her resume, be able to network herself more, and ultimately to reach her super objective which is, *to make a name for herself and live an extraordinary life.* Wicker is composed of very tightly woven straw to get its texture, which is reminiscent of Val. Valerie is very strong performer. She knows what to say to Zach and when to say it. She talks the talk, but she can also walk the walk because she embodies so much talent, which in turn makes her performances very tight and clean.

A sound that perfectly fits Val is "sizzling," for several reasons. First of all, a sizzle is, "a hissing sound in or as if in burning or frying." The sound itself is exciting and draws people's attention. As soon as someone hears something sizzling on the stove, they go over to check it out. This is true for Val. As soon as she starts her story with her monologue and song, she is consistent and never falters and people hear what she has to say and are intrigued. She does not go too far and say too much, like Judy for example, but she gives just enough to make her a valid candidate for the job. This, in turn, is true for sizzling too. When something is sizzling, in a skillet for example, people aren't concerned that it is burning and ruining their dinner, but they are aware that it is cooking the meat just enough. Also, sizzling describes Val in the fact that she is hot. She is a top choice performer and a great candidate for the job, as well as being physically attractive. Sizzling is also described as a hissing sound, which can exemplify Val and Sheila's cat fights. There is a little static and jealousy in the audition between Sheila and Val that never turns into a full flame because they are both professionals and would not let anything get that far.

An arrow is a shape that matches the character of Val because it is direct, and it can also, in the literal sense, be used as a weapon. While Val has the texture of wicker and has that quality about her that looks can be deceiving, she is, on the other hand, very direct and open and is not afraid to tell Zach about her life, or answer any other questions he asks her. Valerie realizes that she should not be ashamed about herself and the experiences that have led her to where she is today. With this being said, in the actual audition, she is open and gives Zach just enough about her life so Zach knows that she does actually care and is trying to get the job. If she did not give enough information, then Zach might think that she does not take this as seriously as he does, and if she gave too much information then she might be shooting herself in the foot. Valerie acts very professional and honest at the same time, which is possibly one reason why she does in fact get the job at the end. The shape of an arrow can also be used as a weapon, just as the shape of Val's body and personality are weapons that Val uses against her competition to get the job. She knows she is younger than Sheila, and she makes a point to let everyone know that and use that against Sheila. Valerie also knows that looks are just as important, if not more important, than talent in show business, so she gets all of this surgery done and then uses that sex appeal and knowledge, more so than some of the other girls, to show Zach how much she wants the job and what she has gone through to get jobs like the one she is auditioning for.

Pepper jack cheese is a food that represents the essence of Valerie Clark quite accurately. Val is not a submissive character in any way, but she will give you what you want and ask for. This pleasing quality about her stems from the fact that her other occupation is, or at least was, a stripper; she gives Zach what he asks for, her story, with no complaints or hesitations, and also because she changed her whole physical appearance so that she would be pleasing to directors' eyes. The same is true for pepper jack cheese. It is a hot, spicy cheese that gives you that satisfaction and craving that you desire from the moment you look for the words "pepper jack" on the package. The embellishments of spicy peppers, especially jalapenos, are an added bonus to regular cheese that won't disappoint you and will deliver on its promises. The same is true for Valerie Clark. She is a spicy little number that comes with talent, brains, and beauty. With all of these embellishments she has, it is no wonder that she made the final cut.

When it comes to animals, "[o]ne of the most ostentatiously adorned creatures on Earth, the peacock uses its brilliant plumage to entice mates." Peacocks are very proud, showy, beautiful creatures that flaunt their beauty to get what they want. Sounds like Val, right? Even Val's stance on the line embodies that cocky feel that a peacock has. Technically a peacock is only the male bird, while peahens are the female birds, which also suits Val because she is very aggressive. Before her transformation, she was a peahen, which is not as decorative and appealing as a peacock, but once she had plastic surgery, she became this beautiful, aggressive creature. It is not that Valerie is full of herself, but she knows what weapons she has, and now that she has them, she might as well use them. The iridescent tail of a peacock "can spread out in a distinctive train that is more than 60 percent of the bird's total length." So, in other words, the beautiful, showy feathers are the characteristics that get peacocks the most attention. This is analogous to Val where her looks are a main reason why she is getting shows now. Before, when her dance skills outweighed her looks, she was not getting into any shows. Now, her appearance (tail feathers) is the highlight of the package that she is selling to directors, and her transformation is her ticket to the stardom that she craves.

Purple is the color that most suits Val. The character of Val is usually seen in purple and I never even thought about why that is until I had to sit down and actually think what color Val is. Purple is perfect because purple is a very regal color that is associated with people of a higher power. Val does not have the highest power or social status during the audition because Zach holds that position, but she does have that majestic sense to her that makes her seem almost untouchable. Sheila does try to cut her down, especially when she criticizes her breast size, but that does not get to Val. She realizes that she is not there to make friends, but rather to do business and get the job. Purple is also a very feminine color, which is appropriate for Val because she loves being a woman. She "fixed the chassis" by having her breasts, nose, butt, and various other body parts done so she could look more feminine and be considered for roles like a "[d]ebutante, chorus girl, or wife." The regal color of purple parallels Val's personality; the essence she possesses, and her outward appearance, all in one.

A firework is a dynamic object based on the fact that it is not alive, does not have a conscience, and it moves. A firework is technically an explosive device, triggered by something, that produces a striking display of loud noise and light. Valerie Clark is a firework in a sense that once Zach opens the floor for all of the dancers to talk about his/herself, Val takes this opportunity and runs with it. She is explosive in her story, her word choice, and in the way she stands and presents herself. She has that "look at me" quality about her that captures a lot of people's attention and makes them want to see more. Valerie has her one moment to shine and step forward and tell her story, and during those five minutes or so, Zach and the audience learn a great deal about the character of Val. Her story explodes on them, and when she is finished, they are left with that dazzled, eager look in their eyes wanting more because she is so entertaining.

Valerie Clark, one of the seventeen dancers on the line, is a very memorable and loveable character because of her specific personality. In my analysis, some words that embody Val are; wicker, sizzling, an arrow, pepper jack cheese, a peacock, purple, and a firework. Human beings are not all straightforward. They have many layers to them that they share with certain people and not others. Valerie Clark is a very complex, interesting character, as you can tell from the words that represent her. She is a very strong woman who is a star to the audience, even if she is only auditioning for a chorus role. This assignment helped me attach myself to the character of Val more, and also allowed me to make some choices about the character that were my own and not previously set in stone.

Rebecca Barczak, University of South Dakota

Chapter 8: Central Production Metaphor

Example: *Arms and the Man*

In the appendix for chapter five we discussed the protagonist's character spines for *Arms and the Man*. You might like to review that analysis before reading the matrix and thematic statement used in the same production.

Central Production Metaphor: *Arms and the Man* is a fractured fairytale.

Thematic Statement: In *Arms and the Man*, Shaw demonstrates that when it comes to love and war, we're all children. Underneath our adult masks, we hide our childlike selves. War is a dangerous illusion, adults playing at cowboys and Indians — but the consequences are real and devastating. The romantic fables that make up our "master narratives" are destructive to us as well as others. And yet … romance beckons even the most resolute realist (and realists are usually disillusioned idealists).

Notes from Director's analysis:

Raina and Sergius are trying to live out the fairytale of romance and heroism. Bluntschli & Louka fracture Raina's & Sergius's false self-images, allowing the real person to emerge.

Which fairytale? Look for ones which involve soldiers. The Louka-Sergius subplot reminds me of "Cinderella," the poor girl saved by the Prince. Ask actors to find or create a fairytale that serves as a "life script" for their character — a variant on a character biography.

The general style is somewhat Brechtian. Strange things happen, "fractures" breaking the illusion for a moment, reminding the audience they are in a theatre watching a play. Brecht intended this sudden shift in perspective to make the audience think critically about what they are watching. In this case, the "fractures" make the audience think critically about Shaw's targets: romantic illusions of love and war.

The scenery evokes a fairytale world, perhaps a mixture of folktale and reality. Same with costumes. An operetta was made of this play, and the costumes should look a bit theatrical, like operetta costumes. There needs to be a moment in each act in which something on the set "fractures," breaking the illusion.

Oh, I just had an image of another kind of "fracture": a little man bringing on a sign that says, *"and they lived happily ever after …"* but too soon, and the stage manager keeps sending him back into the wings — then has to call for him at the right time. Maybe this interruption occurs once in each of the first two acts. The "right time" would be at the very end of the show. Two little men perhaps? We can develop comic business for them, such as one berating the other: "I told you that wasn't our cue!"

Because of the references to opera in Act I — and the operetta version of the play — I'm thinking about having Raina sing some of her idealistic lines. Sergius could sing heroic lines too … and the short romantic scene between Sergius and Raina could become an operatic duet. These "fractures" would remind the audience that the two romantic lovers have chosen as role models theatrical characters, not real people.

Appendix B

The following pages contain Peer Review Checklist forms to be used with the Capstone Assigments at the end of Chapters 2 through 8.

Chapter 2: Given Circumstances

Peer Review Checklist: Given Circumstances

1. **Given Circumstances**

    ___ Includes thorough analysis of all four categories: who, what, where, and when.

    ___ Essay describes major characters and their relationships with other characters

    ___ Essay describes social institutions and groups influencing the characters

    ___ Essay describes where the various parts of the story occur

    ___ Essay describes when each part of the story takes place

    ___ One or more categories is under developed (specify)

    ___ One or more categories is missing (specify)

    ___ Choices accurately reflect what is actually in the script rather than assumptions or inventions

    ___ Includes a summary of the world in which the story "lives"

2. **Organization**

    ___ Sound organizational strategy with an original or interesting approach

    ___ Logical and coherent organization

    ___ Acceptable organizational pattern

    ___ A different organizational pattern would have been more effective

    ___ Totally lacks organization

    ___ Paragraphs lack internal organization

    ___ Paragraphs fail to develop a clear, specific topic sentence

3. **Style**

    ___ Writing is clear, attractive and individual

    ___ Writing has a hint of individuality or inspiration

    ___ Writing is acceptable

    ___ Writing is problematic

      ___ Writing is unclear   ___ Writing lacks vitality
      ___ Writing is awkward   ___ Writing is wordy

4. **Ideas**

    ___ Ideas are engaging and insightful; illuminating insights into the subject

___ Some good ideas; a spark of originality
___ Ideas are acceptable
___ Insight does not go beyond the obvious
___ Random, undeveloped ideas

5. **Supporting Evidence and Arguments**
___ Major points are supported by strong evidence
___ Major points are supported acceptably
___ Major points are not always supported by strong evidence
___ Major points are unsupported

6. **Mechanics (Diction, Grammer, Spelling)**
___ No errors
___ Few distracting errors; see notations on manuscript
___ Some errors; see notations on manuscript
___ Multiple major errors; see notations on manuscript

7. **Purpose (Fulfillment of the Assignment)**
___ Fulfilled the assignment in an imaginative and original way
___ Fulfilled the assignment satisfactorily
___ Fulfilled the assignment only partially
___ Demonstrated script had been carefully read
___ Made interesting use of concepts and terminology discussed in textbook

General Comments:

Chapter 3: Action and Structure

Peer Review Checklist: Structural Analysis

1. **Structural Analysis Outline** (*check all those that apply; explain problems in "comments" section*)

  ___ Beginning stasis clearly identified

  ___ Inciting incident clearly identified and shows how it triggers main action

  ___ Each major complication numbered and clearly identified (both trigger and heap)

  ___ Triggers and heaps of major complications are actions, not feelings.

  ___ Triggers are what antagonists do; heaps are what protagonists do.

  ___ The major crisis is clearly identified and justified; the protagonist's choices are clearly explained as well as the effect the major crisis has on the structural climax

  ___ The major structural climax is clearly identified and justified as *the single moment* that resolves the main action of the story.

  ___ The choice of major structural climax is near the end of the script.

  ___ The major emotional climax is clearly identified and justified *as the single moment of* emotional intensity for the audience

  ___ The new stasis is clearly identified

  ___ The analysis as a whole is unified; the main action is traced through all the structural elements

2. **Organization**

  ___ Logical and coherent organization

  ___ Acceptable organizational pattern

  ___ A different organizational pattern would have been more effective

  ___ Totally lacks organization

3. **Style**

  ___ Writing is clear, attractive and individual

  ___ Writing has a hint of individuality or inspiration

___ Writing is acceptable
___ Writing is problematic
   ___ Writing is unclear   ___ Writing lacks vitality
   ___ Writing is awkward ___ Writing is wordy

4. **Ideas**
  ___ Ideas are engaging and insightful; illuminating insights into the subject
  ___ Some good ideas; a spark of originality
  ___ Ideas are acceptable
  ___ Insight does not go beyond the obvious
  ___ Random, undeveloped ideas

5. **Supporting Evidence and Arguments**
  ___ Major points are supported by strong evidence
  ___ Major points are supported acceptably
  ___ Major points are not always supported by strong evidence
  ___ Major points are unsupported

6. **Mechanics (Diction, Grammer, Spelling)**
  ___ No errors
  ___ Few distracting errors; see notations on manuscript
  ___ Some errors; see notations on manuscript
  ___ Multiple major errors; see notations on manuscript

7. **Purpose (Fulfillment of the Assignment)**
  ___ Fulfilled the assignment in an imaginative and original way
  ___ Fulfilled the assignment satisfactorily
  ___ Fulfilled the assignment only partially
  ___ Demonstrated script had been carefully read
  ___ Made interesting use of concepts and terminology discussed in textbook

General Comments:

Chapter 4: Root Action Statement

Peer Review Checklist: Root Action Statements

1. **Root Action Statement (Thesis)** (check all those that apply; explain problems in "comments" section.)

 ___ Effective root action statement; meets all the criteria

 ___ Problems with root action statement; does not meet all the criteria:

 ___ Does not contain all four parts

 ___ Does not go beyond story level; work on abstracting

 ___ Does not correspond with the script well; read the script more closely

 ___ Main action should be stated as a strong active verb

 ___ Needs work to unify the interpretation in the statement

 ___ Unclear

 ___ The third part of the RAS should correspond with the major crisis of the script

 ___ The "result" part of the root action should correspond with the structural climax of the script

 ___ Other (specify)

2. **Structural Analysis**

 ___ Beginning stasis clearly identified

 ___ Inciting incident clearly identified and shows how II triggers main action identified in RAS

 ___ Each major complication numbered and clearly identified (both trigger and heap)

 ___ Triggers and heaps of major complications are actions, not feelings.

 ___ Triggers are what antagonists do; heaps are what protagonists do.

 ___ The major crisis is clearly identified and justified; the protagonist's choices are clearly explained as well as the effect the major crisis has on the structural climax

 ___ The major structural climax is clearly identified and justified as *the single moment* that resolves the main action of the script

 ___ The choice of major structural climax is near the end of the script

___ The major structural climax corresponds with the result of the RAS

___ The major emotional climax is clearly identified and justified *as the single moment of* emotional intensity for the audience

___ The new stasis is clearly identified

___ The analysis as a whole is unified; the main action identified in RAS is traced through all the structural elements

3. **Style**

___ Writing is clear, attractive and individual

___ Writing has a hint of individuality or inspiration

___ Writing is acceptable

___ Writing is problematic

    ___ Writing is unclear   ___ Writing lacks vitality

    ___ Writing is awkward ___ Writing is wordy

4. **Ideas**

___ Ideas are engaging and insightful; illuminating insights into the subject

___ Some good ideas; a spark of originality

___ Ideas are acceptable

___ Insight does not go beyond the obvious

___ Random, undeveloped ideas

5. **Supporting Evidence and Arguments**

___ Major points are strongly and clearly justified

___ Major points are supported acceptably

___ Points are not always supported

___ Major points are unsupported

6. **Mechanics (Diction, Grammer, Spelling)**

___ No errors

___ Few distracting errors; see notations on manuscript

___ Some errors; see notations on manuscript

___ Multiple major errors; see notations on manuscript

7. **Purpose (Fulfillment of the Assignment)**

___ Fulfilled the assignment in an imaginative and original way

___ Fulfilled the assignment satisfactorily
___ Fulfilled the assignment only partially
___ Demonstrated script had been carefully read
___ Made interesting use of concepts and terminology discussed in textbook

General Comments:

Chapter 5: Tools for Character Development

Peer Review Checklist: Character Spines

1. **Spines (Thesis)** (check all those that apply; explain problems in "comments" section.)

___ Choices meet criteria for effective spines: strong, actable, specific verb choices with psychological insight.

___ Choices do not meet all criteria:

___ Choices do not go beyond story level; need to probe deeper into character.

___ Spines are not stated in infinitive verb phrases

___ Verbs are not strong, actable, and active

___ Spines should be more specific to the character

___ You need spine verbs that can be directed at any character in the script.

___ Reconsider which verb is the strategic and which is the goal spine

___ Other (specify):

___ Clear explanation of *how* the spine choices will stimulate your creativity as an actor

___ Clear identification of spine trigger

___ Spine trigger meets criteria

___ Choices do not meet spine trigger criteria

___ Trigger not appropriate to trigger the spines

___ Trigger not plausible within the given circumstances of the story

___ Trigger not helping you empathize with the character

___ Trigger will not assist in playing the spines

2. **Organization**

___ Sound organizational strategy with an original or interesting approach

___ Logical and coherent organization

___ Acceptable organizational pattern

___ A different organizational pattern would have been more effective.

___ Totally lacks organization

___ Paragraphs lack internal organization

___ Paragraphs fail to develop a clear, specific topic sentence
___ Letter demonstrates pursuit of character spines
___ Letter does not demonstrate pursuit of character spines

3. **Style**
___ Writing is clear, attractive and individual
___ Writing has a hint of individuality or inspiration
___ Writing style in letter captures the character's voice
___ Writing is acceptable
___ Writing is problematic
   ___ Writing is unclear   ___ Writing lacks vitality
   ___ Writing is awkward ___ Writing is wordy

4. **Ideas**
___ Ideas are engaging and insightful; illuminating insights into the subject
___ Some good ideas; a spark of originality
___ Ideas are acceptable
___ Insight does not go beyond the obvious
___ Random, undeveloped ideas
___ Effective use of character biography
___ Letter could contain more significant biographical choices

5. **Supporting Evidence and Arguments**
___ Major points are supported by strong evidence
___ Major points are supported acceptably
___ Major points are not always supported by strong evidence
___ Major points are unsupported
___ Spines are not justified by evidence from the text
___ Analysis does not take given circumstances into consideration

6. **Mechanics (Diction, Grammer, Spelling)**
___ No errors
___ Few distracting errors; see notations on manuscript
___ Some errors; see notations on manuscript
___ Multiple major errors; see notations on manuscript

7. **Purpose (Fulfillment of the Assignment)**
   ___ Fulfilled the assignment in an imaginative and original way
   ___ Fulfilled the assignment satisfactorily
   ___ Fulfilled the assignment only partially
   ___ Demonstrated script had been carefully read
   ___ Made interesting use of concepts and terminology discussed in textbook

General Comments:

Chapter 6: Scenic Units

Peer Review Checklist: Scenic Units

1. **Choice of Objectives** (check all that apply; explain problems in "comments" section.)
   ___ Strong, specific, actable verb choices
   ___ Choice of objectives reveals probing insight into character psychology and interactional patterns
   ___ Probe more deeply beneath surface action
   ___ Work for stronger, more specific, actable verbs
   ___ Both tactical and goal objectives appropriate
   ___ Reconsider which is the tactical and which the goal objective
   ___ Objectives must be stated in infinitive verb form
   ___ You need an objective for each character in each unit, whether or not the character speaks in that unit
   ___ You need to use infinitive verb *phrases* to clarify meaning

2. **Cause of Change**
   ___ Clearly defined
   ___ Choices show psychological insight
   ___ Unclear how trigger causes heap
   ___ Unclear how CC causes a change in motivational pattern
   ___ List cause of change as change into following unit

3. **Choice of Where to Divide Units**
   ___ Clearly defined
   ___ Choices show psychological insight
   ___ Some units could use further division
   ___ Too many teeny-tiny units; divide into larger chunks
   ___ Choices unclear

4. **Format**
   ___ Follows sample
   ___ Unit analysis needs to be on pages facing text, to make easily readable/usable for actor/director
   ___ Messy presentation

5. **Mechanics (Diction, Grammer, Spelling)**
   ___ No errors

___ Few distracting errors; see notations on manuscript

___ Some errors; see notations on manuscript

___ Multiple major errors; see notations on manuscript

6. **Purpose (Fulfillment of the Assignment)**

___ Fulfilled the assignment in an imaginative and original way

___ Fulfilled the assignment satisfactorily

___ Fulfilled the assignment only partially

___ Demonstrated script had been carefully read

___ Made interesting use of concepts and terminology discussed in textbook

General Comments:

Chapter 7: Thematic Statements

Peer Review Checklist: Thematic Statement

1. **Thematic Statement (Thesis)** (check all that apply; explain problems in "comments" section.)
   ___ Effective, insightful, stimulating thematic statement that meets all the criteria
   ___ Problems with thematic statement; does not meet all the criteria
   ___ Incorrect format.
   ___ Unclear
   ___ Doesn't appear justifiable based on what happens in the script
   ___ May not include all essential elements of the play.
   ___ Too general
   ___ Work for more insight
   ___ Too close to cliché
   ___ Unlikely to stimulate artistic creativity.

2. **Root Action Statement** (used to justify thematic statement)
   ___ Effective RAS; meets all the criteria
   ___ Problems with RAS; does not meet all the criteria:
   ___ Does not contain all four parts
   ___ Does not go beyond story level; work on abstracting
   ___ Does not correspond with the script well; read the script more closely
   ___ Main action should be stated as a strong active verb
   ___ Needs work to unify the interpretation in the statement
   ___ Unclear
   ___ Other (specify)

3. **Organization**
   ___ Sound organizational strategy with an original or interesting approach
   ___ Logical and coherent organization
   ___ Acceptable organizational pattern
   ___ A different organizational pattern would have been more effective
   ___ Totally lacks organization

___ Paragraphs lack internal organization
___ Paragraphs fail to develop a clear, specific topic sentence

4. **Style**
    ___ Writing is clear, attractive and individual
    ___ Writing has a hint of individuality or inspiration
    ___ Writing is acceptable
    ___ Writing is problematic
        ___ Writing is unclear   ___ Writing lacks vitality
        ___ Writing is awkward ___ Writing is wordy

5. **Ideas**
    ___ Ideas are engaging and insightful; illuminating insights into the subject
    ___ Some good ideas; a spark of originality
    ___ Ideas are acceptable
    ___ Insight does not go beyond the obvious
    ___ Random, undeveloped ideas

6. **Supporting Evidence and Argument**
    ___ Major points are supported by strong evidence
    ___ Major points are supported acceptably
    ___ Major points are not always supported by strong evidence
    ___ Major points are unsupported
    ___ No RAS

7. **Mechanics (Diction, Grammer, Spelling)**
    ___ No errors
    ___ Few distracting errors; see notations on manuscript
    ___ Some errors; see notations on manuscript
    ___ Multiple major errors; see notations on manuscript

8. **Purpose (Fulfillment of the Assignment)**
    ___ Fulfilled the assignment in an imaginative and original way
    ___ Fulfilled the assignment satisfactorily
    ___ Fulfilled the assignment only partially
    ___ Demonstrated script had been carefully read
    ___ Made interesting use of concepts and terminology discussed in textbook

General Comments:

Chapter 8: Central Production Metaphor

Peer Review Checklist: Central Production Metaphor

1. **Thesis Statement/Statement of Purpose** (check all that apply; explain problems in "comments" section.)
   - ___ Well-articulated and appropriate metaphor
   - ___ Problems:
     - ___ You don't have a central production metaphor
     - ___ Your production metaphor isn't really a metaphor
     - ___ Your metaphor doesn't fit with your thematic statement
     - ___ Your metaphor doesn't contribute new insight into the story
     - ___ Your metaphor is unlikely to stimulate creativity
     - ___ Your metaphor doesn't help unify the production
     - ___ Your metaphor is just a historical period, done for novelty's sake, bizarre, a classification of what the play is, or a metaphor for a character rather than the play
     - ___ Other problems

2. **Organization**
   - ___ Sound organizational strategy with an original or interesting approach
   - ___ Logical and coherent organization
   - ___ Acceptable organizational pattern
   - ___ Not all ideas are clearly related to the production matrix
   - ___ A different organizational pattern would have been more effective
   - ___ Totally lacks organization
   - ___ Paragraphs lack internal organization
   - ___ Problems with paragraph organization; paragraphs fail to develop a clear, specific topic sentence

3. **Style**
   - ___ Writing is clear, attractive and individual
   - ___ Writing has a hint of individuality or inspiration
   - ___ Writing is acceptable
   - ___ Writing is problematic
     - ___ Writing is unclear   ___ Writing lacks vitality
     - ___ Writing is awkward ___ Writing is wordy

4. **Ideas**

___ Ideas are engaging and insightful; illuminating insights into the subject

___ Some good ideas; a spark of originality

___ Ideas are acceptable

___ Insight does not go beyond the obvious

___ Random, undeveloped ideas

___ Design decisions could be more specific

5. **Supporting Evidence and Arguments**

___ You have used the tools of script analysis to justify your choice of metaphor

___ You have used the tools of script analysis to justify your design choices

___ Major points are supported by strong, concrete evidence

___ Major points are supported acceptably

___ Points are not always supported by strong evidence

___ Major points are unsupported

___ No clear, complete thematic statement to support your choice of metaphor

6. **Mechanics (Diction, Grammer, Spelling)**

___ No errors

___ Few distracting errors; see notations on manuscript

___ Some errors; see notations on manuscript

___ Multiple major errors; see notations on manuscript

7. **Purpose (Fulfillment of the Assignment)**

___ Fulfilled the assignment in an imaginative and original way

___ Fulfilled the assignment satisfactorily

___ Fulfilled the assignment only partially

___ Demonstrated script had been carefully read

___ Made interesting use of concepts and terminology discussed in textbook

8. **Use of Visual or Aural Materials**

___ Visual aids vividly communicated your design concept

___ Visual aids helped to communicate your design concept

___ Visual aids could have been better selected to communicate your design concept clearly.

General Comments:

Glossary

Abstraction: A thinking process which starts at the level of reality—the specific and concrete—and moves to the level of concepts.

Actable Verbs: Infinitive verbs that are clear, strong, appropriate and as specific as possible to the character and situation.

Action: The key to script analysis; something a character does consciously that is significant to the outcome of the story.

Activity: An insignificant "doing" that does not require thought.

Analogy: Often described as a comparison between two linked pairs on the basis of relationship. In mathematics, an analogy might be expressed as follows: A : B :: C : D. An example of an analogy stated in words: hand is to fingers as foot is to toes. Analogy is so foundational to the process of human thinking that philosophers have difficulty defining it.

Analytical Thinking: Separating a phenomenon into its essential parts in order to understand its deeper meaning and how it works.

Antagonist: A character who opposes the protagonist.

Artistic collaborators: A team of theatre artists whose work transforms a script into a play.

Beginning Stasis: The situation at the beginning of the script. Represents a "balance" about to be "unbalanced."

Bird's Eye View: A "macro-centric" perspective useful for uncovering themes and patterns.

Cause of Change (CC): The trigger and heap that cause a character to change tactics in a scenic unit.

Central Production Metaphor: A concise, overarching metaphor that synthesizes the analytical work of script analysis and reveals the essence of the interpretation; it guides all creative decisions by the artistic team.

Character Biography: An acting technique in which an actor creates a backstory for the character. The actor begins with given circumstances in the script but invents a complete life for the character.

Character Spine: The main goal the character is pursuing throughout the whole script.

Close Reading: A method of reading requiring attention to detail and relationships; designed to reveal structure and deeper meaning of a piece of literature. Requires multiple readings of the text under examination.

Commitment: In William Perry's highest stages of critical thinking, an individual acknowledges uncertainty and relativity but makes her own choices about what to believe based on personal values, critical thinking, supporting evidence, and having compared different disciplines and their criteria.

Complications: Anything a character other than the protagonist does that affects which way the story's main action develops. Can be in the form of an obstacle or unexpected help.

Conflict: A clash between two opposing forces. Drama is based on conflict.

Constantine Stanislavski (1863-1938): Russian actor/director and founder of modern acting theory.

Constructive Critique: Honest feedback designed to enhance a product or process, pointing out both strengths and weaknesses of the current effort in an encouraging manner.

Contextual Relativism: The third developmental stage in William Perry's theory of stages of critical thinking. A worldview that acknowledges the importance of considering a particular situation and which criteria fit that situation; those criteria can then be used to evaluate one's answers to questions and problems. Developmental stage in which critical thinking is first utilized.

Convergent Thinking: Problem solving through traditional methods of logic and research when one "right" answer is expected.

Creative Thinking: Synthesizing diverse elements in new and useful ways.

Crisis: a choice point; the moment when a character must choose what action to take next in order to resolve a complication.

Criteria: A set of standards, tests, or rules for evaluating the quality or validity of something.

Critical Thinking: Evaluating the validity of a conclusion or process based on disciplinary or situation-specific criteria which serve as standards for assessment of the process used or conclusion reached.

Divergent Thinking: Generating a lot of potential solutions for an open-ended problem which may have a number of possible answers.

Dualism: The first developmental stage in William Perry's theory of stages of critical thinking: A worldview based on the concept that all things are either "right" or "wrong." Dualism depends heavily on the primacy of authority.

Empathy: Identification with or vicarious experiencing of the feelings of another.

Ending Stasis: A new state of balance at the end of the story.

Exposition: Information about circumstances occurring before the start of the script but essential for the audience to understand what happens.

Given Circumstances: The physical, social, and psychological environment in which a story takes place.

Goal Objective: One part of a unit objective; what the character wants in the moment.

Goal Spine: One part of a character spine; what a character most wants to do.

Ground: A description of characteristics the topic and vehicle of a metaphor have in common.

Habits of Mind: A disposition or attitude signaling intelligent behavior when a person is confronted with a problem to which he does not have a ready answer, such as paradoxes, dilemmas, enigmas and uncertainties.

Heap: An event that occurs in response to a preceding trigger.

Higher Level Thinking Skills: Thinking that requires the thinker to do more than accumulate, identify, and reiterate knowledge. Analytical, critical, and creative thinking are higher level thinking skills.

Inciting Incident: The significant trigger that sets the main action of the story (heap) in motion. The "tipping point" that "unbalances" the stasis.

Infinitive Verb: An indefineable verb form that is nonetheless essential to the process of acting. In English the basic verb is preceded by "to," as in "to act," "to attack," "to defend," etc.

Inner Monologue: An acting exercise during which actors explore what their character is thinking but not saying. It reveals the subtext of dialogue. The actor speaks the thoughts "as if" the character were thinking, e.g., "Ugh! I hate that dress you're wearing!" rather than in third person, e.g., "My character doesn't like the other character's dress."

"Inside Out" Acting Technique: Exploring a character by analyzing the internal, or psychological, actions that fuel a character's external actions.

Interpretation: The guiding vision that communicates to an audience an artistic team's understanding of what the script shows about the meaning of human life.

Main Action: The most significant action the protagonist pursues throughout the entire play.

Major Complication: Anything a character other than the protagonist does that affects which way the story's main action goes.

Major Crisis: The turning point when the protagonist must make a choice that leads to the ending of the story.

Major Dramatic Question: A question which arises in the audience's mind at the inciting incident: what will be the outcome of the action? This question may undergo changes as the script progresses, usually rising to higher levels of significance.

Major Emotional Climax: The single moment that is the emotional highpoint of the story for the audience.

Major Structural Climax: The single moment when the protagonist does something that resolves the main action.

"Magic If": An acting tool that bridges the gap between the actor and the character; the actor uses the given circumstances of the story to ask, "How would I behave if I were this character in this situation?"

Mental Management: Thinking about how you think and guiding your own thinking

Metacognition: Thinking about the way you think.

Metaphor: A mental construct comparing two seemingly unrelated phenomena in order to reveal that they share some common characteristics.

Mindfulness: Paying conscious attention to how you do something.

Multiplicity: A worldview, the second of William Perry's developmental stages, that acknowledges differing perspectives regarding right and wrong but does not apply criteria or critical thinking to resolving disagreements. If there is no one right answer then all answers must be equally valid.

Obstacle: Anything that prevents the protagonist from completing his/her main action.

"Outside In" Acting Technique: Explores the character with kinesthetic thinking to get a "feel" for the character, starting with physicality rather than psychology.

Paradigm Shift: A major change in the protagonist's belief as to how the world works, usually based on a significant discovery.

Peer Review: Feedback from a friend, colleague, or classmate.

Play: The performed interpretation of the script.

Protagonist: The main character of the story. It is the protagonist's story that is being portrayed.

Raisonneur: The voice of reason; a character who reveals the playwright's point of view. In some scripts, several characters may share this function.

Reflection: Contemplation of one's choices and processes.

Root Action Statement (RAS): A single sentence which summarizes your view of the script's main action.

Scenic Unit: Small slice of a scene in which a character's tactic and goal objectives remain the same.

Script: A special kind of writing that tells a story; it is purposely incomplete and requires a team of artistic collaborators who complete the storytelling through visual and aural designs, acting, and directing.

Script Analysis: A method designed to decode the script in ways that help theatrical collaborators make artistic choices.

Spine Trigger: The most essential part of a character biography that explains the origin of the need which the character attempts to fulfill by pursuing his spine goal.

Stage Directions: Parenthetical statements in a script describing given circumstances, movement or motivation. They may be authored by the playwright or by someone connected with the script's first production.

Story Level: Looking at the individual narrative in the script without seeing its universal implications.

Strategy spine: One part of a character spine; the way a character goes about getting what he wants.

Structural Analysis: Taking a script apart to reveal the larger building blocks of its underlying foundation.

Tactic Objective: One part of a unit objective; the way the character goes about achieving his moment-to-moment goal.

Target: One part of a unit objective; the subject of your character's tactic.

Thematic Statement: A complete sentence that describes your interpretation of the story's meaning.

Thematic Subjects: Topical threads that are woven into the texture of a story.

Topic: One part of a metaphor; its qualities are less well-known than the vehicle's.

Transitive Verb: A verb that requires an object upon which to act.

Trigger: An event that causes a responding event, called a heap.

"Triple Threat" Thinking: The ability to think analytically, creatively, and critically as well as recognize situations when each will be useful.

Unified RAS: All four parts of the RAS must relate to each other in a causal manner.

Unit Objectives: What characters do moment to moment in a scene, in pursuit of their character spine.

"Valid" interpretation: Grounded in what is actually happening in the script.

Vehicle: That part of a metaphor that transfers, or carries over, its qualities to the topic.

World of the Play: A synthesis of the given circumstances in which the story takes place.

Worldview: The overall perspective from which one sees and interprets the world; a mental model of how the universe works.

Worm's Eye View: A "micro-centric" perspective. Good for discerning details, internal-structures, and relationships.

Bibliography

Austin, James H., M.D. *Chase, Chance, and Creativity: The Lucky Art of Novelty.* Cambridge, MA: MIT Press, 2003.

Ball, David. *Backwards and Forwards.* Carbondale, IL: University Press, 1983.

Ball, William. *Sense of Direction: Some Observations on the Art of Directing.* New York: Drama Book, 1984.

Birken, Marcia, and Anne C. Coon. *Discovering Patterns in Mathematics and Poetry.* Amsterdam: Rodopi, 2008

Black, George. *Contemporary Stage Directing.* Chicago: Holt, Rinehart and Winston, 1991.

Bronson, Po and Ashley Merryman. "The Creativity Crisis." http://www.newsweek.com/2010/07/10/the-creativity-crisis.print.html Internet; accessed 27 July 2010.

Brookfield, Stephen D. *Developing Critical Thinkers: Challenging Adults to Explore Alternative Ways of Thinking and Acting.* San Francisco: Jossey-Bass, 1987.

Burch, Milbre. "Holding Up the Sky." Unpublished script. Columbia, MO, 2009.

Caine, Renate Nummela, and Geoffrey Caine. *Making Connections: Teaching and the Human Brain.* Menlo Park, CA: Addison-Wesley, 1994.

__, Geoffrey Caine, Carol McClintic, and Karl Klimek. *12 Brain/Mind Learning Principles in Action: The Fieldbook for Making Connections, Teaching, and the Human Brain.* Thousand Oaks, CA: Corwin, 2005.

Cameron, James. Director/Writer/Producer/Editor. *Avatar.* Feature film, Twentieth Century Fox, IMAX 3D, 2009.

Cameron, Julia. *The Artist's Way.* London: Pan, 1995.

Carr, Nicholas. *The Shallows: What the Internet Is Doing to Our Brains.* New York: W. W. Norton, 2010.

Clurman, Harold. *On Directing.* New York: Simon and Schuster, 1971.

Costa, Arthur and Bena Kallick. "Describing 16 Habits of Mind,"
    http://www.habits-of-mind.net/ Internet; site last revised 19 January 2008; accessed 7
    October 2008.

Csikszentmihalyi, Mihaly. *Creativity: Flow and the Psychology of Discovery and Invention.*
    New York: Harper, 1996.

Darling-Hammond, Linda, Brigid Barron, P. David Pearson, Alan H. Schoenfeld,
    Elizabeth K. Stage, Timothy D. Zimmerman, Gina N. Cervetti, Jennifer L. Tilson.
    Powerful Learning: What We Know about Teaching for Understanding. San Francisco:
    Jossey-Bass, 2008.

Dunlosky, John, and Janet Metcalfe. *Metacognition.* Los Angeles: Sage, 2009.

Ellis, Arthur K. *Research on Educational Innovations*, 4th ed. New York: Eye on Education,
    2005.

Gressler, Thomas H. *Theatre as the Essential Liberal Art in the American University.*
    Studies in Theatre Arts, 16. Lewiston, NY: Edwin Mellon, 2002.

Grote, David. *Script Analysis: Reading and Understanding the Playscript for Production.*
    Belmont, CA: Wadsworth, 1985.

Hartman, Hope J., Ed. *Metacognition in Learning and Instruction: Theory, Research, and
    Practice.* Dordrecht: Kluwer, 2001.

Hetland, Lois, Ellen Winner, Shirley Veenema, and Kimberly M. Sheridan. *Studio
    Thinking: The Real Benefits of Visual Arts Education.* NY: Teachers College Press, 2007.

Hodge, Francis. *Play Directing: Analysis, Communication, and Style.* 5th ed. Boston: Allyn
    and Bacon, 2000.

Holton, Orley I. *Introduction to Theatre: A Mirror to Nature.* Englewood Cliffs, NJ:
    Prentice-Hall, 1976.

Holyoak, Keith J., and Robert G. Morrison, Eds. *The Cambridge Handbook of Thinking
    and Reasoning.* Cambridge MA: Cambridge University Press, 2005.

___, and Paul Thagard. *Mental Leaps: Analogy in Creative Thought.* Cambridge, MA: MIT
    Press, 1995.

Horstman, Judith. *The Scientific American Brave New Brain.* San Francisco: Jossey Bass, 2010.

Immordino-Yang, Mary Helen, and Lesley Sylvan. "Admiration for Virtue:
    Neuroscientific Perspectives on a Motivating Emotion." *Contemporary Educational
    Psychology* 35 (2010): 110-15.

___, and Kurt W. Fischer. "Neuroscience Bases of Learning." In *International Encyclopedia
    of Education*, 3rd ed., ed. V. G. Aukrust; Learning and Cognition section. Oxford,
    England: Elsevier, publication forthcoming.

___, and Antonio Damasio. "We Feel, Therefore We Learn: The Relevance of Affective and Social Neuroscience to Education." *Mind, Brain, and Education,* 1, no. 1 (2007): 3-10.

Jackson, Norman, Martin Oliver, Malcolm Shaw, and James Wisdom, Eds. *Developing Creativity in Higher Education: An imaginative curriculum.* New York: Routledge, 2006.

___. "Imagining a Different World." In *Developing Creativity in Higher Education: An imaginative curriculum,* ed. Jackson *et al.,* 1-9.

Johnson, Andrew. *Up and Out: Using Creative and Critical Thinking Skills to Enhance Learning,* Boston: Allyn & Bacon, 2000.

Koestler, Arthur. *The Act of Creation: A study of the conscious and unconscious in science and art.* New York: Dell, 1964.

Kurfiss, Joanne G. Critical Thinking: Theory, Research, Practice, and Possibilities. ASHE-ERIC Higher Education Report No. 2. Washington, DC: The George Washington University Graduate School of Education and Human Development.

Leamnson, Robert. *Thinking About Teaching and Learning: Developing Habits of Learning with First Year College and University Students.* Sterling, VA: Stylus, 1999.

Longman, Stanley Vincent. *Page and Stage: An Approach to Script Analysis.* Boston: Pearson, 2004.

May, Rollo. *The Courage to Create.* New York: W.W. Norton, 1975.

Moore, Sonia. *The Stanislavski System: The Professional Training of an Actor.* 2nd rev ed. New York: 1984.

National Leadership Council for Liberal Education & America's Promise. *College Learning for the New Global Century: Executive Summary with Employers' Views on Learning Outcomes and Assessment Approaches* [LEAP Report]. Washington, DC: Association of American Colleges and Universities, 2008. Available from http://www.nxtbook.com/ygsreprints/ygs/p14594_aacu_nxtbook/#/2; Internet; accessed 19 September 2010.

Nelson, Craig E. "On the persistence of unicorns: The tradeoff between content and critical thinking revisited." In *The Social Worlds of Higher Education: Handbook for Teaching in a New Century,* ed. B.A. Pescosolido and R. Aminzade. Pine Forge Press, 1999.

Nickerson, Raymond S., David N. Perkins, and Edward E. Smith. *The Teaching of Thinking.* Hillsdale, NJ: Lawrence Erlbaum, 1985.

Paivio, Allan, and Mary Walsh. "Psychological Processes in Metaphor Comprehension and Memory." *Metaphor and Thought,* 2nd ed., ed. Andrew Ortony, 307-28. Cambridge, MA: Cambridge University Press, 1994.

Perry, William G., Jr. *Forms of Intellectual and Ethical Development in the College Years: A Scheme*. New York: Holt, Rinehart, and Winston, 1970.

Ritchhart, Ron, Mark Church, and Karin Morrison. "Putting Thinking at the Center of the Educational Enterprise," pre-publication version of Ch. 2 from *Making Thinking Visible*, used with permission of the authors for the Harvard Project Zero Future of Learning Institute, August 2010.

Root-Bernstein, Robert, and Michèle Root-Bernstein. *Sparks of Genius: The 13 Thinking Tools of the World's Most Creative People*. Boston: Houghton Mifflen, 1999.

Rowe, Kenneth Thorpe. *A Theater in Your Head: Analyzing the Play and Visualizing its Production*. New York: Funk & Wagnalls, 1960.

Runco, Mark A., Ed. *Critical Creative Processes*. Creskill, NJ: Hampton, 2003.

Sanders, Donald A. and Judith A. Sanders. *Teaching Creativity Through Metaphor: An Integrated Brain Approach*. New York: Longman, 1984.

Shaw, George Bernard. *Arms and the Man*. New York: Samuel French, 2009.

Sternberg, Robert J., Ed. *Handbook of Creativity*. Cambridge, MA: Cambridge University Press, 1999.

___, and Elena L. Grigorenko. *Teaching for Successful Intelligence: To Increase Student Learning and Achievement*. Arlington Heights, IL: Skylight, 2000.

Thomas, James. *Script Analysis for Actors, Directors, and Designers*. Boston: Focal Press, 1992.

Toporkov, Vasily Osipovich. *Stanislavski in Rehearsal; The Final Years*. Translated by Christine Edwards. New York: Theatre Arts Books, 1979.

Tishman, Shari, David N. Perkins, and Eileen Jay. *The Thinking Classroom: Learning and Teaching in a Culture of Thinking*. Boston: Allyn & Bacon, 1995.

Waxberg, Charles S. *The Actor's Script: Script Analysis for Performers*. Portsmouth, NH: Heinemann, 1998.

Weimer, Maryellen. *Learner-Centered Teaching: Five Key Changes to Practice*. San Francisco, CA: The Josey-Bass Higher and Adult Education Series, 2002.

Wilshire, Bruce. *Role Playing and Identity: The Limits of Theatre as Metaphor*. Bloomington: Indiana University Press, 1982.

Zull, James E. *The Art of Changing the Brain: Enriching the Practice of Teaching by Exploring the Biology of Learning*. Sterling, VA: Stylus, 2002.